Knot for Keeps

Sathya Saran is one of India's best-known journalists and editors. As editor, she made *Femina* the most successful fashion and lifestyle magazine in India. She is author of the critically acclaimed and bestselling biography *Ten Years with Guru Dutt: Abrar Alvi's Journey*, as well as the bestselling biographies of S.D. Burman and Jagjit Singh. She has also authored a short-story collection titled *The Dark Side*. Sathya's popular column in *Femina* 'From Me to You' is running as a guest column in *Dainik Jagran* even now. She is currently working on a number of books as consulting editor with HarperCollins India.

Knot for Keeps

Writing the Modern Marriage

edited by

SATHYA SARAN

HarperCollins *Publishers* India

First published in India by
HarperCollins *Publishers* in 2018

Building 10, Tower A, 4th Floor, DLF Cyber City, Phase II,
Gurugram Haryana – 122002, India
www.harpercollins.co.in

P-ISBN: 978-93-5277-911-6
E-ISBN: 978-93-5277-912-3

Typeset in 11/14.2 Sabon LT Std at
Manipal Digital Systems, Manipal

Printed and bound at
MicroPrints India, New Delhi

Contents

Introduction ix
Sathya Saran

(... about love not in partnership, but as a part apart...)
Apportionments of Love 1
Sharanya Manivannan

(... on marriage ... being not necessarily a good thing!)
Conjugular 12
Chitra Viraraghavan

(... on love ... in sickness as in health...)
A Life Sentence 22
Rita Mukherjee

(... you win some, you lose some...)
Heaven Forbid 29
Krishna Shastri Devulapalli

(... on the rough road to the perfect relationship...)
रिश्तों की डगर है मुश्किल 40
प्रसून जोशी
Rishton Ki Dagar Hai Mushkil 41
PRASOON JOSHI

(... Can she say 'khula' to his 'talaq'?)
Keep Searching, a Light Might Appear 44
NOOR ZAHEER

(... on twenty-three years of remote-controlled togetherness...)
Our Bi-continental Marriage 58
KALYAN RAY

(... a long and short story...)
The Imperfect Marriage 65
HARIMOHAN PARUVU

(... on breaking stereotypes...)
Marriage and Me 76
DEEKSHA NAGAR

(... on being civil and civil marriage in India...)
The Cost of a Runaway Marriage 90
NEHA DIXIT

(... when Bengal loves Punjab...)
Mixed Media Marriage 108
BULBUL SHARMA

(... on parting ways with tradition...)
The Thin Red Line 116
MODHURIMA SINHA

(... on desperation in the late twenties...)
A Girl of a Certain Age 123
ABHA IYENGAR

(... when Law plays the villain...)
Across Latitudes and Longitudes 134
WENDELL RODRICKS

(... a few of my favourite things...)
What I Hate Most 139
MILAN VOHRA

(... on the New Indian Marriage...)
Sacrament, Contract or Relationship? 145
VIJAY NAGASWAMI

About the Contributors 155

Acknowledgements 161

Introduction

Sathya Saran

This is an anthology on marriage.

But then, what is marriage?

A marriage is a bond between two people. It might indeed be made in heaven, but has to be conducted on earth.

Marriage is a partnership between equals. If both partners understand this, they can create a little heaven.

Marriage is a balancing act. Sometimes one side is heavy, at other times the other. In such instances of asymmetry, it is required that there be complete understanding, so the balance can be restored to mutual benefit.

Marriage is communication. It requires talks, gestures and many small but significant signs that all go a long way to help navigate the long road of togetherness, which often hits rough patches and tough times. Communication keeps the carriage moving – it is the oil that lubricates the wheels through the journey.

Marriage is understanding. That both can be right and wrong at the same time. That there is more than one point of view. That Mars and Venus were terms coined by an astute mind to make this simpler to understand.

Marriage is never going to bed angry, a rule that has saved many a relationship.

Marriage is the courage to admit a mistake, the ability to say sorry.

Marriage is sharing, caring, growing together. Learning from falls and mistakes, and not blaming the other even if they are blameworthy.

Marriage is never saying 'I told you so'.

Marriage is not licence to ignore, or take the other for granted.

Marriage is not a house with walls of silence dividing the partners.

Marriage is not a game of one-upmanship.

Marriage is not a social media event.

Marriage is not romance and roses. It is a gift richer and more lasting, that needs constant care to keep growing.

Marriage is not the beginning of happily ever after. It is the first step towards making 'ever after' happy indeed.

And of course marriage is more. Much more...

So, here then is a collection of stories, essays, thoughts and perspectives on marriage. Reading it can be fun – it can make you laugh, cry, sigh or rejoice. Much as being married makes us do...

Apportionments of Love

Sharanya Manivannan

One day, at the beginning of the year that I turned twenty-four, I wept terribly as I came to terms with the knowledge that I would never be a young mother, the thing I had wanted all of my life. When my birthday arrived a few months later, I spent most of it with a couple who did not want me to be alone that day. At some point that afternoon, I leaned over or looked down during our conversation in a garden café, and noticed how one's big toe softly caressed the other's. They were both smiling, and a feeling of having intruded flared in me: Even when keeping me company, they were alone *together*, whereas I was alone solely. As I write this, eight years have passed, but I have not forgotten the memory of accidentally sighting their feet casually grazing one another's under the table, and how it made me feel.

This much deeper into an unpartnered life, this is the second thing I must tell anyone who wonders how this paradigm is possible – the ache will not go away.

But before that, here is the first thing I must tell anyone about finding a meaningful paradigm for an unpartnered life: It is possible.

Why should the natural state of the adult human being be partnership?

Let me be very clear. To reject marriage is not the same as to reject partnership. There are plenty of people in committed partnerships who prefer not to marry for any number of reasons – legal, ethical, emotional and otherwise. But to be unpartnered despite the desire for it, even with political sensibilities that critique the institution, is an experience of its own. The sharply honed critique does not fill certain voids; it does not put its arm around you as you sleep; it cannot slow-dance with you or hold your hand on a turbulent plane. But what it does is recalibrate your own sense of self-worth and how you move in the world, what you make possible for yourself – and for others.

To arrive at the state of non-partnership as a socio-political tool, one must work backwards, beginning with the interrogation of the institution of marriage. There is extensive feminist literature on the same, which tackles not just the deeply problematic nature of heteronormative household dynamics but also everything from sexist etymology (did you know the English word 'husband' has its roots in agriculture, from Old Norse words that meant someone who owned and tilled land, the woman being a part of his property, and from which the term 'husbandry', as in 'animal husbandry', comes from?) to the clear-cut sexism of many ceremonial wedding customs we are now conditioned to think are romantic. Each patriarchal culture has its own set of specificities. In India, the practice of dowry despite its criminalization and the continuing legality of marital rape are but two.

The deep intertwining of marriage and sexuality must also be challenged. Consider the absurdity of the term 'pre-marital sex'. What is that except the presumption that sex before marriage is out of the norm because marriage is an eventuality? These are not theoretical issues – not when you're a sexually active woman in need of gynaecological attention, for example. Chennai – the city I live in and, significantly, spent my twenties in – is notorious for pharmacies refusing to stock emergency contraceptive pills. There is no logic to it besides moral shaming.

The profound shame of being a sexual woman, that shame deeply enforced by family, peer groups, one's own lovers, random strangers, workplaces, authorities and organizations of all kinds – how that doesn't radicalize more people into feminism, I do not understand.

Heterosexual cis-men benefit from marriage, a fact even health studies have proven. Is it in their best interests to challenge the institution? I would argue that it is. Subjectively, to have more equal partnerships is to have a richer life, and more broadly, to contribute to social justice is also to have a more meaningful life. But for women, the interrogation of matrimony and the prevailing systems it is built on and sustains is more than just a cerebral or experimental exercise. It is necessary for the survival of the sovereign self. Unpartnered or otherwise.

When I was five years old, my father reprimanded me gently once: 'If this is how you disobey your father, is this what you will do, when you grow up, to your husband?' I hung my head and said, 'I don't want a husband then.' I remember this so clearly. It was a moment of awakening, of dual clarity – about what it meant to be a wife, and about how certain I was that I didn't want such a role for myself. And as vexed as I have been by some of my failures in affairs of the heart, I also know there was never a time when I carried myself otherwise. I wear this like a scar on the chest, at once a matter of pride and a terrible wounding.

In India, seven decades since the end of British colonial rule, we like to think both love and feminism are Western imports, and are wrong on both counts. To work towards a homegrown political consciousness about the problematic institution of marriage, it is B.R. Ambedkar we must go to first. In a paper delivered at Columbia University, in 1916, called 'Castes in India: Their Mechanism, Genesis and Development', he said, 'As for myself I do not feel puzzled by the Origin of Caste in India for, as I have established before, endogamy is the only characteristic of Caste and when I say *Origin of Caste* I mean *The Origin of the Mechanism for Endogamy*.' In fact, he quite clearly elucidated the following: 'I regard endogamy as a key to the mystery of the Caste system.' In this concise paper, one of the few points that hasn't aged is about the practice of sati, which Ambedkar delineates using a theory about 'surplus' women and men, about widowers being allowed to continue their sexual and household lives, while widows were killed or at best ostracized, explicitly showing in a local context the sexist (if not misogynistic) bedrock of the institution. All the rest of it, unfortunately, remains relevant.

A 2016 report from the National Council of Applied Economic Research found that only 5 per cent of Indian marriages are inter-caste. What this means is so obvious that it hardly requires explanation. For all our pretensions about progressiveness, for all our insistence that we believe in love and romance, the vast majority of Indians ultimately marry and mate in ways that confirm and perpetuate prejudices.

My theory of modern, particularly urban and middle- and upper-class, marriage in India can be explained with the fire trampoline analogy.

Picture it. The pleasure of having, of setting alight, many flames – followed by a skilled escape. Pseudo-liberalism allows for it: sex and dating, even full-fledged relationships, with an expiry date implied. No accountability is expected, and there may be a reward for bad behaviour. In other words, you can set a person's house – or heart – on fire, jump off into the safety net you knew was waiting for you, look up and shout, 'I always told you I'd marry a woman/man of my parents' choosing!'

In tandem with the fire trampoline is that oxymoron, the arranged-cum-love marriage. The aspirational spin of romance put on the basic set-up of orthodoxy. A round of applause for the bride and groom, for the coincidence of falling in love within their sub-caste, for the coincidence of their matching birth charts, for the coincidence of how feudal it all seems (but it is only a coincidence, they shrug).

The mythologist Joseph Campbell, in his iconic conversation with Bill Moyers, spoke of marriage as a form of spiritual union. Among other things, he said, 'When you make a sacrifice in marriage, you're sacrificing not to each other but to unity in a relationship. The Chinese image of the Tao, with the dark and light interacting – that's the relationship of yang and yin, male and female, which is what a marriage is. And that's what you have become when you have married. You're no longer this one alone; your identity is in a relationship. Marriage is not a simple love affair, it's an ordeal, and the ordeal is the sacrifice of ego to a relationship in which two have become one.'

To paraphrase, if I have understood correctly, if you put the idea of being married, with its vast manner of contents and conveniences, as the foremost thing, if you aligned to it conceptually instead of adapting it to your subjective nature, you could basically make it work. I understand the romance of this idea, but I am alarmed by its fatalism. I think in particular of one man who looked like the sky had fallen on him in his wedding photographs, who I watched affirm repeatedly and to all and sundry how much he and his wife – his 'chosen' one, his ordained consort – were in love with each other. It's not an unfamiliar story. 'Say it long enough and maybe you'll believe it too,' I hissed sardonically (out of earshot) at first – until I realized that it was true. He had chosen to be married. The *to whom* was incidental. The *why* was a mystery I conferred theory upon theory, and turned over and over like a pebble in a pocket. The *how* is the thing I cannot picture at all – the tedium of partnering, coupling and co-parenting without true love and respect.

This is why we are wrong to begin an original dismantling and reassembling of the institution of marriage from the angle of sex, even though it seems to be the most logical one. It seems logical only because orthodox marriage is held to be the beginning of sexual activity, a milestone that is artificial in nature – and in fact, contrary to nature. But the discussion or performance of sexual liberation alone is insufficient if one ultimately still relies on and tiptoes around the security – perceived or otherwise – of the institution. We must begin instead with the less apparent, the most deeply insidious and systematic, that comfort zone within which our immediate needs are taken care of as long as we perform the role adequately, be it groom or bride, father-in-law or new mother. Which is to say that before we begin to reshape the world, we must begin with ourselves.

I said earlier that a sharply honed critique cannot make up for a lack of partnership, particularly the physical and practical aspects of the same. But what it can do is firmly contextualize an unpartnered person as being a challenge to existing hegemony.

To be single can be radical, if one has enough of both self-awareness and empathy to be so. There is a now archetypal idea of the independent, unpartnered woman, largely fashioned through American television shows. She is outspoken. She has no qualms about spending her hard-earned money on what pleases her. She invests her time in her friendships and career, and seeks romance, but only in parallel to an already full life. She is sexually liberated.

I raise a toast to this epitome (and we know she'd never turn down a toast, particularly if it were in the form of a pink martini), which paved many a great path, but I also offer a fresh, indigenous archetype. Let me try and describe her, this blueprint for an unpartnered woman of this century. She is as compassionate as she is passionate. She considers her privilege, and seeks to equalize it, so that more people can benefit from and access the routes she has been able to choose or pave for herself. She identifies ontologically with the Other without appropriating from them. She always considers the larger framework, be it the environment or the imagination. And yes, she buys her own jewellery. Yes, she lusts; yes, she travels alone. But that's not all. That cannot, in so insular and hegemonic a time and place, be any more than the first impression.

When you rub up against the friction of a society that seeks to put you in what it deems to be your place every day, you'd be surprised how easy it is to become this woman.

I wish I could say that it is as easy to become that man, her perfect equal. But like for pearls-in-oysters and diamonds-in-coal, there has to be enough rub or pressure to create them, which is simply not there within the mechanism of heteropatriarchal society. That often leaves the independent woman more independent still.

My parents had a film-style 'love marriage'. They met in a medical college in Madras in the 1970s. He walked out of his family and abandoned his significant inheritance, taking a passport for the first time to go to her home in Sri Lanka to ask for her hand after close to a decade of courtship. He married into her family, incidentally the custom of the matrilocal, matrilineal society she came from on the east of the island. My family had that bafflingly intriguing mixture of conservatism and lack of convention that many highly dysfunctional ones do.

Suffice to say that my sisters and I were raised neither to know we could seek out and find love, nor to expect matrimony to come to us on a platter – approved and arranged; with betel leaves, vermillion powder and a sweet.

Have I wanted to marry? Yes, yes. Despite cautionary tales, despite intelligence, despite defiance, the conditioning is hard to shake loose. You fall in love and don't realize how unthinkingly, how artlessly, you also fall in step with that trajectory, the idea that marriage follows love as hour follows hour.

But it was only for one year of my life that I really wanted it – in abstraction, without a locus of love in sight. In hindsight, I was at exactly the age (the rockstar's treacherous twenty-seven) when most people make that decision, fearing societal disapproval and biological ticking clocks, although my reasons for it were darker. Bewildered, severely traumatized and in need of restructuring my entire life, I tried to put myself on some path that was not as untrodden as the one I'd always known. I complied to the remedies that organized religion and the marriage-minded offered. In Tamil Hinduism, there are two kinds: the veynduthal and the pariharam. Veynduthals are votives; pariharams neutralize karmic complications. Doing the latter, you ask for absolution. Doing the former, you simply ask. I did a number of both things that year, obediently traipsing to temples with my parents, who, themselves bewildered, were only obediently traipsing along too. Varied prophecies, proved patently false, accompanied these expeditions. Not a single such entreaty worked, and in the few years that followed, my disappointments were compounded by how they seemed to work for almost everyone else. Including, most painfully of all, some of the objects of my affection. You don't need to believe in the institution of marriage in order to be devastated by a beloved's wedding.

There is a temple on the East Coast Road in a village called Thiruvidanthai, where Vishnu is Nithyakalyana Perumal – the Eternal Bridegroom. This temple is the ultimate failsafe for Hindu Tamils seeking matrimony; able people of all genders and ages participate in a ritual meant to expedite the same. The ritual consists of the following: Two garlands are bought and given to the priest at the sanctum sanctorum; one garland is given to the Lord, and the supplicant puts the other one around their neck and circles the temple nine times; this worn garland is then stored safely in one's home, and its wearer brings it back to the temple with their partner once their marriage has been solemnized.

I have heard only two stories in which the supplicatory ritual has not yielded a wedding within months. One story belongs to one of my closest friends. The other is, of course, mine. I remember distinctly the December dusk in which I performed those circumambulations, as M.S. Subbulakshmi's unmistakable voice on the speakers cantillated the 1008 names of the presiding deity. It was a beautiful hour to be in a 1,300-year-old temple. The garland I wore that evening hung in my home's prayer room for a while. I believe my mother kept it in a drawer somewhere when it began to parch into potpourri. It must be dust by now. Flower dust. I don't mean that as a metaphor at all.

Let me tell you about remedies.

For a glitch in the seventh house of your horoscope, wear a rose behind your ear. For the shame the 'settled' force upon you, swallow tea steeped so long that the bitterness dreamed itself sweet. For jealousy, dance to music set to lyrics in a language you cannot understand except with your body. When that body reminds you it has neither homed a nestling ever nor a lover in so long, rub the violet grains of a kernel of pearl millet between your fingers and let the wind take them from you. On the day when the one who has currently leased your heart ties the knot around someone else's throat, place your feet in seawater. Watch the tide venture and recede over the silver you bought yourself: nuptial toe-rings, belled anklet vines. For the way it feels to fall asleep alone, fill the spaces you lodge in with the scent of bergamot. For long celibacy, bare your arms to the light as often as possible; let the sun sing to your skin. In this and all seasons, learn to love the singe.

Oh, and finally – the only cure for love is love.

—w—

It's been a long time since I thought of the word *yuanfen*, but I was once shattered by the concept. I remember nothing else about the novel I came across the Chinese word in as a teenager, except that it was explained as something like this – the apportionment of love one is meant to have. I have come to accept, not without rue, that in my life this apportionment of mine is both smaller in dimension and larger in nature than I ever imagined it could be.

The human heart has a capacity beyond comprehension, and it can proffer just as much as it can hold. It regenerates. That no one has come to fill my heart in a certain way, that it has sometimes felt diminished by all those who sipped from it but did not stay, changes nothing about its nature. One learns love as a verb and as a state – in work and in art, in dialogue and in altruism, at home and in the world.

—w—

Those divorced after long marriages, and those who raise children on their own after having done so with a partner, have different stories to tell. I wonder about that sometimes: to be agreeably embraced by the system and then to either willingly reject it or to grow comfortable with one's rejection from it. I have never wanted, without doubt, to be inside – neither would I likely have been allowed it (for long, anyway). I have no sense of what that is like, for even in my most deferential and devoted apportionments of love, I have always been on the periphery. I would say the same of those I know who were married only briefly, and those who married only for the bureaucratic expediency. I would say the same of those who are partnered, but who resolutely reject heteronormative paradigms of what that should look like. I would say the same of everyone who is queer, especially in situations where it is not safe to be.

But I will also say that there are things no one can know about long loneliness without having lived it. Without the years turning page after page until you stop counting how long it has been since.

But the more I've talked and written about this, about all of the vulnerability and volition of being a romantic who refuses partnership or matrimony for its own sake or on unequal or unhappy terms, the more I've met with people who wanted to be reassured that this too can be a way to live and to love. Deeply. I have hungered for beaten paths too, for things to be easier, to have to explain myself less. In seeking to find a map, not knowing I would have to make so much of it up as I went along, I would like to think that I have at least helped one come into being.

Conjugular

CHITRA VIRARAGHAVAN

If we hadn't been out of the country, Arvind and Roshni would still be together. Which is not necessarily a good thing, if you take my meaning.

Roshni agreed when I met up with her at the local Café Coffee Day. She swirled the grounds in her cup and allowed them to settle and stared down at them as if trying to read the future she had mapped out for herself. 'I did try your number, you know.'

'But you knew we were out of town,' I said, sipping delicately at my green tea and looking at a young couple walk through the door and occupy the table furthest from everyone else.

'... So anyway, my mum was ill ... you know, the usual stuff plus phlebitis ... Would you believe it, the nurse at Mission knocked the drip needle out of her arm, let it fall to the ground and just stuck it back in – so I moved in with them.'

'So how is she? When was this?' I watched the young couple. Give them time, and they would come round, much like everyone else, if you take my meaning.

'Last month,' she said, following my gaze, finding nothing very compelling in its object, and coming back to the grounds.

'And you haven't gone back? Not called?'

Roshni was busy checking her mobile and smiling to herself.

'Hmmm? No.'

'So is there someone else?'

I liked to get right down to it, if you take my meaning.

She stared. 'Well, that's why I called you. See, we went to this party, and I met a guy who I used to know in the leather business, you know. A long time ago, before we were married.'

'And?'

'Well, some man was weird with me at the party, and Arvind did absolutely nothing, can you believe it; and this guy, Kailash, who I told you about? He just goes to the other guy and catches him by the collar...' Roshni's eyes glazed over in equal parts vanity and self-congratulation.

'And?'

'And nothing ... we sort of got involved, you know. But that's over, too. I hate all men. I'm over that phase of my life.'

I watched the young couple leave. Give it time, people, if you take my meaning.

Arvind called one afternoon. 'I need to speak to Vinay,' he said, not expecting me to pick up the phone, which was funny, since I was in our house. 'His mobile is switched off.'

'He's taking a nap. Is it anything?'

'Well ... the thing is ... It's business. Can you ask him to call me?'

Business. Not a word one free-associated with Arvind, one of those fake zamindari types with the cash, the lifestyle, but no life's work. Also, not the fastest draw in the west, if you take my meaning. Okay, the east.

'Roshni has left the house,' Vinay said later.

'So what does that mean? She's left the house or she's left him?'

'She's gone to her parents' house.'

'I know that, she told me,' I said. 'Her mum's been ill.'

'Well, the mother is fine but she isn't back.'

'So what's she saying to him?'

'She isn't. That's why Arvind called. He wants us to go see her.'

'Us?'

'He thought you should be there, too. You know, woman confiding in woman, that type of thing.'

Roshni's parents had a flat given to them by her (correction: Arvind) in a twenty-year-old block, once the height of posh, set right on the Adyar. As we walked through the basement parking, a darkish, unidentifiable fluid eased out of the floor above, competing with the river in rankness. Not a nice place to live in, if you take my meaning.

Roshni didn't seem surprised to see us. 'Arvind sent you, I guess,' she said, reluctantly offering for us to sit down. There was a glassed old-fashioned book cupboard to one side. I tried to read the titles through the rime of dust. The Cliff Notes to *Anna Karenina*. *Physics for Degree Students*. *The Fountainhead*. *The Manorama Year Book 1979*. *Recovery of Faith*.

Roshni noticed my gaze. 'You know how my entire family is into reading,' she said, bridling somewhat, as if suspicious of my intentions.

I smiled at her. The phone rang. She made no move to pick it up. 'Lalitamma!' she yelled, giving us a start. Lalitamma rushed out of the kitchen, wiping her hands on her sari, and grabbed the phone, throwing what seemed to be a resentful look at Roshni.

Over Lalitamma's Shubha Mudgal-on-an-off-day voice, Roshni said, 'I don't pick up the phone. Bound to be for my parents. Why confuse the issue, right? People ask me how long I'm here ... ta da da da da...' When had she picked up that American way of speaking? Must be the fresh blood she was hanging out with, if you take my meaning.

'So how long are you here?' I said.

Vinay nudged me unsubtly. He smiled at Roshni. 'So, how are you? Long time,' he said. 'Is your mother better?'

'I don't know what Arvind's been telling you,' she said. 'I had a polyp in my uterus that needed to be taken out. Did he tell you that? Well, anyway, he refused to even take a look at it when the problem first came up.'

Vinay looked at me and shifted in his seat.

'So I had to go and have it out, you know, at Malar.'

'You should have called us,' I said, trying to look at the books on the bottom shelf. 'How did you go?'

Roshni's parents walked in. Her mother once-overed us, losing interest half-way. Roshni's dad followed his wife inside, no bossman round these parts, if you take my meaning.

'Dad drove me there and back. That was yesterday,' Roshni said, adjusting the vada-shaped bum-seat under her.

An image of the long-lost Kailash came to me. Fine, I had never seen him but I could have an image of him, right? Polyp? It was no damn polyp, if you take my meaning.

'So what did Arvind tell you? Did he tell you we haven't had sex for years? Did he?'

Vinay shifted some more in his seat. I tried to pin down the line of poetry that had been tormenting me since morning. No goddamn luck. A new image came into my head. It was of Arvind crashing his car full of girls, one of whom wasn't Roshni, but one of whom was trying to shift his stick at the time, if you take my meaning. So went the rumour. 'Huh?' I said, trying to keep the conversation going.

'Did he tell you that he was big into porn?'

Vinay looked up at that, and at me. But I had my own issues. 'Huh?' I said, helpful nonetheless.

'He'll try to deny it, let him try!' she said.

'Well, anyway,' Vinay said, 'he wants to meet. You know, talk things over.'

We fixed a place and time. The Hyatt bar, 7 p.m., Saturday. Arvind was there when we got in at 6.55. He was consuming a plate of cold cuts and downing a beer.

'What's this?' said Roshni, walking in, and taking a huge forkful of salami.

'Beer? Anything else?' Arvind said like in the old days.

'Hmmm,' she said, looking through the menu. 'Yes. Could you order the caviar on toast?' She took a swig of his beer, held it in her mouth, considering it. 'Okay, a glass of red. And none of that house wine stuff.'

Arvind grinned at us. Problem solved, he seemed to be saying.

'So, if you like, we'll leave,' Vinay said. 'You guys can chat?'

'No, no, stay, what's the hurry?' Arvind said.

Roshni nodded violently in agreement, not speaking because her mouth was full. Her mother had raised her well, it was obvious.

Well, many glasses of red later, and shandy for me, that meeting was inconclusive, if you take my meaning.

Arvind called one morning. 'She's coming. She texted!'

'What did she say?' I said, examining my nails. I really did need a manicure.

'She wants to come over to get her books. I bet she's only saying that. I bet she really wants to come back but doesn't want to say so outright. You catch my point?'

'But doesn't she say she just wants her books?'

'That's her excuse, don't you see!' he said. 'Where's Vinay, anyway?'

Arvind was like someone with special skills, if you take my meaning. His special skill was being able to interpret insignificant social acts and events in a manner that enhanced his own somewhat obscure sense of things.

Later, Roshni called me. 'I'm going over to get my books. Those are the only things that matter to me, you know. Those, and the case they're in. That's antique, I'll have you know. A family heirloom. I've texted Arvind.'

I imagined the book titles. *The Secret*. The Twilight series. A pristine edition of the *Collected Works of Shakespeare*. *Half Girlfriend*. *Fifty Shades of Grey*. With a bit of luck, *Gone Girl*...

Roshni interrupted my train of thought. 'I'm going there tomorrow.'

'Okay,' I said. 'So how's ... whatsisname?'

'Kailash?' she said, a tad irritable. 'I told you it was over, didn't I? You really should pay attention when people tell you things, Karuna.'

Roshni had her own special skills. They involved living like a lady on someone else's lolly, if you take my meaning. She once told me that she spent her afternoons writing letters in the old-fashioned way at her roll-top desk after the cup of nicely brewed tea and the thin-cut cucumber sandwiches. That Kailash character was probably rich. Someone said he was a breeder of high-end canines.

Arvind called. 'She came and took her books. The dogs were devastated when she left.'

A line of poetry suggested itself to me. 'She left her dogs for a dog breeder...' Well, not exactly a haiku but succinct nonetheless, if you take my meaning.

'What did you say?' he said, morose.

I didn't realize I'd said the line out loud. 'Nothing, nothing,' I said. 'Just remembered something.'

'Well, tell Vinay to call me when he's home.'

There was no news of Roshni and Arvind for some days. Just as we had decided to lead our own lives, if you take my meaning, there was a call from Arvind.

'Where's Vinay?' he said, calling on the landline.

'Out,' I said.

'Well, I can tell you, I guess. See, she's definitely coming back!'

'And you know this how?' God, those kitchen tiles really could do with a wipe-down.

'She's used the credit card to buy stuff at Lifestyle!'

'What stuff?' I said in a tone that showed I cared. I examined my face minutely in the gloss kitchen cupboard doors, feeling a sense of disquiet at the enlarged pores.

'Sixteen thousand rupees' worth of lingerie!' he said. 'Would you believe it?'

'And you know this how?' I said somewhat repetitively, playing for time, turning my face this way and that, and making a moue. Time for a steam and facial.

'The statements come to me, that's how. Where's Vinay?'

But I was with Arvind no longer. I had torn myself away from the cupboard doors and soared on the viewless wings of poesy to Roshni and Kailash in their den of vice, if you take my meaning.

I was jobless one day, so I called Roshni.

'Guess what?' she said. 'I've filed for divorce.'

'Oh?'

'Yes, almost a year is up, you see.'

'So, does Arvind know?' I said.

'Of course he does, silly!' she said. 'In fact, my lawyer is a friend of his parents.'

'A bit of an odd choice, wouldn't you say?'

'No,' she said, expertly combining glee with complacency. 'He knows exactly what they have; that stingy bastard can't cheat me.'

'Hasn't Arvind given you the house your parents live in?' I said for the sake of saying something.

'So what? The least he owes me after all these years of putting up with him!'

Arvind called Vinay. 'She's filed for divorce. I'm filing for restitution,' he said.

'Make it amicable,' Vinay said. 'Why do you want to fight with her? Give her what she wants. You love her, right? You want her back, right?'

I was passing by and heard that bit of the conversation. I pinched myself hard to prevent myself from bursting into a belly-laugh. Love? Arvind? Roshni? That was a bit intense, if you take my meaning.

Vinay ignored me. 'Show her you care. She may even come back to you then,' he said.

'You think?' Arvind said.

'Yes. Do it.'

'There's a lot of stuff in her name she doesn't know about!' Arvind said. 'I'm not going to tell her.'

I lingered, unbeknownst to Vinay.

'Fine, do what you want,' Vinay said. He seemed to be coming around at last to my view of the situation, if you take my meaning.

For days, there was no news. I felt left out of things. I called Roshni. 'How's it going?' I said.

'I bet that cheap bastard made you call me,' she said.

'No, Roshni, why would you think that?' I said. 'Just wanted to see how you were doing, is all. It's been a while.'

'He's been giving me all sorts of trouble,' she said. 'I think I'm being followed.'

'But why?' I said. 'Is it because of Kailash?'

'Kailash! Kailash! I told you I'm not with him any more, didn't I?' she said. 'What's the matter with you?'

'So where are you staying?' I said, trying to change the subject as I practised a pirouette.

'What kind of question is that? With my parents, of course!' she said.

'Funny,' I said, picking myself up off the ground, 'I was trying to call you the other day, your mobile was switched off. So I called your parents. They said you had moved out. But, don't worry, it wasn't anything important. In fact, would you believe it, I've forgotten why I called. Senior moment!'

'Be careful, Karuna,' she said, trying hard to sound friendly, 'maybe you're losing it, if you take my meaning.'

One day, I was so bored, I called Roshni. We met at the Coffee Day. I arrived early and sat where I could see her coming in. A red BMW Sports docked in front. Roshni got out and walked in, looking like the eighty lakhs she had just got, selling off the stocks in her name using a mutual stockbroker friend. She told me this later in the conversation, of course.

'Cool wheels,' I said.

'They're borrowed,' she said. 'From a friend. I had a job interview this morning. With a French company, no less!'

'Oooh, la, la,' I said adverbially. '*Très drôle.*'

She looked at me. 'I'm learning French, too.'

'*C'est magnifique,*' I said, and waited.

Roshni ordered her coffee after careful perusal of the menu with a manicured, gloriously incarnadine nail the exact shade of her stilettos. 'So I sold the stocks in my name,' she said, laughing. 'The bastard didn't know I knew they were in my name. I took them with me when I left!' She laughed some more. 'I'm no fool, you know.'

'I would never think that of you, Roshni,' I said almost sincerely, if you take my meaning.

On our way out, I ran a less-than-manicured nail across the BMW's side. Roshni reacted as though I'd smacked her, with all the nerviness of a new owner, if you take my meaning. 'Please don't do that,' she said. 'My friend just got it.'

'Well, *bonne chance*,' I said adverbially again as I hailed an auto.

She gave me a look and drove off in a blur of red.

Someone told us later that Arvind was numskull-deep in the politics of the Boat Club. The annual general elections were on, and he was very busy campaigning for himself.

Since Arvind and Roshni were doing things other than divorce, I figured it was time for us to move on as well. I had a book to write and had spent pretty nearly all damn year on them. I consoled myself that it was all material, if you take my meaning.

One evening, I was hauling my remains down the beach road when I saw a familiar figure. It was Roshni. She didn't see me. Even I could tell that what she had at the end of a leash was a top-of-the-line pooch.

If you take my meaning.

A Life Sentence

Rita Mukherjee

As my husband and I made our way home from the doctor's clinic that hot and humid day in 2007, Mumbai's cacophony of honking, lane-swerving and snarling up of traffic went on as usual. Everyone seemed to be in a hurry to get to some place. But inside our car there was silence. It was moving at a reluctant pace, not quite wanting us to get home and face the truth of the medical reports, which, lying seemingly innocuous in their file, were more like a death sentence.

I had been diagnosed with idiopathic interstitial pulmonary fibrosis (IIPF) – in layman's language, a scarring of the lung tissue that causes an ever-worsening shortness of breath and a progressive decline in lung function. 'Idiopathic' implies that the cause is still unknown.

Like cancer, IIPF is non-contagious and, so far, non-curable, though research continues to seek causes, cures and ways to manage the disease, which affects three in every 10,000 persons. Like diabetes (which I also have) – it is a degenerative disease.

But unlike diabetes, it cannot quite be controlled by dieting, exercising or doing yoga.

But for some strange reason as we drove home in that silence, and even when we finally arrived, I wasn't thinking of what lay ahead for me … Instead, my mind went into rewind mode, trying to capture and hold close all the good times we'd had together over three decades.

The first time I met him was on a monsoon evening in July. It was closing time at the emporium in Delhi where I worked. He had dashed in more to avoid the drizzle, I suspect, than to buy anything. There were a trillion tiny droplets of rain in his hair and the bright shop lights made them shine like diamonds, giving him a very Mills & Boons hero effect. My Mr Right was born that instant.

The girls at the other counters had already left to spruce up before leaving for home, but I was still putting away the consignment of goods that had arrived a while ago. He came over and asked if we had any unusual cards for birthdays. I showed him the paper-thin filigree leather cards that had just arrived from Shantiniketan. He was happy with his find and after some deliberation chose three. He did not know it then but along with them he also picked up my heart.

After that he made a couple more visits, in fact several more, to tell the truth. Nearing closing time, he would be there waiting on his sturdy black steed, his motorbike. We would grab a cup of coffee and chat and then he would drop me home. This became a regular routine after a point of time. Soon I looked forward to meeting up with him almost every day.

My staid, always-on-the-right-side-of-the-law nature adhered to his impulsive, caution-to-the-winds attitude like a duck to water. Soon I started thinking, after the coffee and chat sessions ended … Now what? I was a great believer in destiny.

He scoffed at it and said man makes his own destiny and should live by the choices he makes.

One evening we met up at a common friend's wedding. His friend from school was getting married to a colleague of mine from work. Needless to say we were delighted to see each other there and sat chatting till the wee hours of the morning. Soon it was time for the 'vidai'. While everyone was bidding the bride, Mala, a tearful goodbye, I watched as he turned to put an arm around my colleague's mother and, soon, made her smile through her tears with his witty comments. One by one he had all of us singing instead of crying. Finally, a cheerful Mala, hugging and kissing us farewell, escorted by her father, went and sat in the car. That day I saw a side of him I had not seen earlier – his ability to get along with folks of all ages (incidentally, he had met Mala's parents for the first time at the wedding) and make light of a serious situation. That got me thinking. After one month, one week and one day, I decided I wanted to spend the rest of my life with him. He loved to talk to me but did he have long-term plans? As they say ... Nothing ventured nothing gained ... So I decided to pop the question to him. Under a star-filled sky, sitting out on the lawn sipping coffee, my knight said yes to me.

His friends and mine were initially surprised because we are very different in so many ways – even in our outlook towards life. My idea of relaxing is to curl up with a hot cup of coffee and a book with an unusual plot or a twist in the tale. His idea is to go with his impulse and, well, just have fun. Like zipping off for a long drive, or spotting a full moon in the middle of the night, or taking off suddenly to a restaurant just to share a cup of coffee together.

But our mutual acceptance of each other brought us together and till today that remains the same. When staid semi-conventional *me* teamed up with fun-loving impulsive *him*, it made a wonderful combo for adventures. But there is much more to him than fun ... There is that dogged determination, tireless hard work and a passion for excellence ... And it took him to the top in his line of work. It is this aspect that breathed new life into me after that 'death sentence'.

While I was going through my sepia-tinted moments, he was furiously researching on the web to know more about lung fibrosis and the possibility of alternative treatments. The findings were not very happy and soon he too slumped into a dark, dismal mood. But after two days of gloom, he sprang back and decided that since we could not wish this ailment away, we just had to 'live' with it and move on in life.

It meant that he was going to give me the best time of my life.

Travel has always been top-most on our bucket list. Now, he decided, was the time for it. For the first time in his working career he took twenty-five days off his accumulated leave, in the year 2008, and we set off for New Zealand. We toured both the North and South islands by road. It was summer in New Zealand and we soaked in the beautiful weather which was so different from summer in Mumbai, Delhi, or Hyderabad – the places we had lived in after marriage. I celebrated my birthday on the first of our trips ... It will always be my most memorable one.

On our return from New Zealand, he continued searching the web for answers, trying to find out ways to slow down the degeneration and make my downhill slide less traumatic. A friend told us about an ayurveda hospital in Coimbatore. My pulmonologist in Mumbai gave me the go-ahead to start ayurveda and yoga, even as I continued my allopathic treatment of steroids to manage the illness.

And so I met the wonderful Dr Ravindran, whose holistic treatment almost miraculously helped stall the degeneration and literally gave me a new lease on life. We have since the first time made the annual, and sometimes semi-annual, trip to Coimbatore for the past several years, making it as much a holiday, with a detoxifying and rejuvenating regime, as it was a treatment option.

Despite it all, we continued to travel every year. To the Sundarbans to see the royal Bengal tigers (maybe they would vanish before I do); to America (multiple trips to visit our daughter studying there); to the United Kingdom – memorably to the Lake District, to the Bard's house; to Spain to see Picasso's world, Flamenco dancers, and the fabulous architecture; to Egypt, Jordan, Israel. To revisit Goa, Varanasi, and Odisha.

And when we returned home from each trip, he wouldn't give me the option of brooding. In fact, I realized that my own attitude had changed. I too wanted to do it all … live every moment. I revived my latent writing skills. I took up searching the web again for unusual recipes with ordinary ingredients. I started living again.

IIPH hasn't left me – it won't because it is as determined as my husband! I am on an oxygen machine 24/7. Again, thanks to his research and relentless efforts, these are mobile units, as convenient as possible given the circumstances. They allow me to lead a life that is almost normal and now even my family and friends just take the paraphernalia that accompanies me as an extension of myself.

Left to myself, I would have resigned myself to fate. It is entirely through the efforts of my life partner that I live to tell my tale. Whenever I slumped, he helped me up and taught me to live in the here and now. As the Bard said so wisely: '… Sweet are the uses of adversity … They teach us sermons in stone…'

Any kind of sickness, whether ordinary or life-threatening, needs a support system beyond medicines and doctors. You also need a constant supply of positive thoughts. My favourite quote – 'Two men looked out of prison bars. One saw mud, the other stars' – is so apt when we view the many diseases or challenges we have to accept and tackle in our lives.

In our marriage, I guess, I am the one who tends to look at the mud and he at the stars … Or perhaps he just creates his own stars. My husband believes that every problem has a solution if you only look hard and long enough. If it isn't in the box, he will just step outside the box to look for it.

I take a no at face value and stay resigned to fate. I sometimes think we have travelled this far in our marriage because he doesn't quite know the meaning of 'No, it can't be done'. It could be tackling my disease, or driving to Goa for a pre-booked holiday on the Mumbai–Goa highway which was closed due to a landslide on *that* day. Unlike others who turned around, we made it, much to the surprise of the hotel staff who had only seen cancellations that morning!

I would never have ventured out of my comfort zone if it hadn't been for him. Or now, my discomfort zone. But in spite of my ailment hanging over our heads, he keeps planning trips, making sure that we are taking the shortest route and the most comfortable mode of transport to get there. Everything is executed to a T.

When we get into marriage, we think of adjustment, of accommodating another individual's life or food habits, religious views, his/her choice of books and music and a million other things. I have learnt that attitude is the most important, and a sense of humour goes a long way to make light of all the problems that visit us at every stage of life.

Any disease – and especially a life-threatening one – has this capacity to chip away at your sense of humour too. It is difficult to talk when you can hardly breathe; it is even more difficult to laugh! And, as time passes, I have to stop doing some of my favourite things (cooking … not advisable to go into a kitchen with your oxygen tube like a thin, elephant's trunk up your nose), making me more cantankerous. So, despite knowing that losing my temper is bad for me and that patience is the least I can pay him for all he continues to do to make my life easier, I do tend to fly off the handle ... But then almost four decades of marriage does give you practice in handling such situations!

Like every other couple, we have had our share of volatile arguments, days (sometimes weeks) of angry silence and belligerent disagreements. But in the end we sort it out, calming ourselves to think of the other's point of view ... and get on with life.

'Get on with life' takes on a new meaning in one's sunset years, especially when one partner has a disease without cure ... But, with a rare courage and determination, he is honouring the most important of the wedding vows: 'To have and to hold in sickness and in health.' In the end, irrespective of which partner bids adieu first, it is the memories of the relationship and romance that help carry that lone individual forward till the final curtains come down.

Heaven Forbid

Krishna Shastri Devulapalli

That it wasn't the average November became apparent when I received my eleventh invitation. It was Margazhi the following month – the time Chennai turned into a burbling cauldron of classical dance, bondas and NRIs, but even so. I hadn't hurt anyone. Why me? Ten of the invites had come value-added with corn-syrupy phone calls from the performer herself. Telling us how the presence of aesthetes like ourselves meant everything, and did we know any 'amenable' journalists capable of writing gushing reviews, by the way? Of these calls, two were from women I don't remember ever having met. And one from someone I suspect wasn't a woman at all in the complete sense.

After ducking six or seven of these like a suicidal IPL player having misgivings after betting on his own decapitation, I was forced to take one right in the chin. It was from the wife of a classmate. One of the few fellows I'd actually liked in school. He was now a doctor in Dallas – an oncologist who'd been steadily, and profitably, seeing Stetson-d cowpokes off to that big Bar & Grill in the sky for over twenty years.

'You will come, won't you?' he said. Even over the phone, his anguish was palpable.

'Sure, da, wouldn't miss it for the world,' I said even as my wife hit me repeatedly on the head with the invitation that had been hand-delivered by a smiling flunkey a couple of days earlier. That it was the size and weight of a leather-bound law book didn't help. (Except, instead of leather, it was Kanjeevaram silk.)

Time: Two days after recital.

Venue: A very expensive bar.

Vishwa Sattiraju, my friend who looked more patient than doctor, swallowed his second whisky in one efficient, if discourteous, gulp.

'Ever wished you were a pauper?' he said. The Argus-eyed waiter had already brought him a refill.

'Not really,' I said. Considering I'd settled last year's milk dues only yesterday, I had no immediate romantic need to be broke. I ordered another whisky. Just to be on the safe side.

'I wish I was, da,' he said.

'Why?' I said. I wasn't aware that the Sri-Sri-Juggy-Chopra-New-Age bug had left the confines of the Bay Area and was afflicting hardened Texans.

'You know how much this whole dance-vance-shindig of Priya's cost me?' he said.

The mention of his wife's name brought back memories of two days ago – something we had so far managed to blur with overpriced whisky – like a kick to the testicles.

Vishnu Gana Sabha: The auditorium is packed from first row to last. From the buzz, you could be forgiven for thinking it was a T.M. Krishna–Sunny Leone jugalbandi instead of a dance ballet written, directed and principally performed by an unknown dancer from George W. Bush's native state. The audience, I slowly realize, as the wife hits me ritually on the head with the invite, constitutes the following categories: immediate family of danseuse, immediate family of children who are accompanying danseuse, the clueless, the bribed, the blackmailed, the threatened, the suicidal, the masochistic, and a couple of fugitives from justice looking for an interim air-conditioned hideout.

—w—

'Not really. How much?' I said.

Vishwa pulled a pen out of his pocket, scribbled on a soggy napkin and slid it across to me. I looked, expecting a number. What I got instead was a pretty evocative doodle of one unmentionable male part and two hirsute, if asymmetric, subsidiaries thereof.

'An arm and a leg, I guess,' I said.

'Yes,' he said. 'Inserted up my ageing buddankadonk … repeatedly.'

I couldn't help but notice that Vishwa's vocab, unlike in our Vidya Vihar days, had acquired something of a personality.

—w—

Priyadarshini Sharma Sattiraju stood perfectly still. All ninety-three kilos of her, except for the jiggly bits heeding Newton's First Law. Around her, a group of hapless NRI kids and a couple of white American ones collided with each other on stage in what was meant to be a colourfully symmetric formation when visualized in her studio in the US. She held her pose. It would have looked like the standard pose of all Nataraja idols except that her raised leg was being held up by one petrified white kid who was slowly turning blue. It was quite obvious that it was less out of Gurubhakti than fear of being trampled to death. A voice in the background explained the delicate nuances of the poignant scene from the two-hour-long ballet in a Bronx-meets-Besant Nagar accent. That the scene was supposed to convey through dance Shakuntala's divine love for Dushyant came as a surprise. To my untrained eye, it was as good a depiction of Emperor Ashoka renouncing everything after the Kalingan bloodbath as I'd ever seen.

—w—

'She runs a dance school, you know?' Vishwa said. 'Yes,' I said, shuddering a little.

How could I forget her invitation-cum-biography featuring her school?

Nritya Canyon
Texas's Only Certified School of Bharatapudiattam

'She has ninety-odd students, each paying her a monthly fee of hundred dollars,' he said.

The latent pawnbroker in me, the one that would've done fabulously well had he been born in Sowcarpet, did, as the Yanks say, some math. My buddy was talking ten thousand smackeroos – that, too, cold, hard tax-free USD. I would've volunteered for waterboarding for less.

'So it's not all bad,' I said.

'Worse,' he said.

'What do you mean?'

'*She* charges hundred bucks. *I* pay the parents one hundred and fifty, without her knowledge ... so they continue sending their kids to her school,' he said.

Did I detect a tiny sob? 'Why?'

'Just to keep her off my back, da. Nearly fifteen thousand dollars ... every month. I don't know how long I can keep this up.'

—w—

It was the end of the programme. The clock said two hours had passed. It felt like Lawrence of Arabia. Not so much the film as his life. As if we had lived it. His desert years, at least. A couple of audience members exited on wheelchairs. Had they come in walking? I couldn't be sure. Priyadarshini stood at the centre of the stage receiving large floral bouquets, one after the other, with a tremendous smile on her crater-free moonface. An assistant ticked off names on a notepad. He was making sure the florist that Vishwa had paid in advance at dollar rate wasn't doing them out of a couple of bouquets. Two men with high-tech movie cameras trained their lenses on the principal dancer. One, running around the danseuse to get a circular-trolley effect. The second, hanging upside down, maybe not entirely by design, from a crane. Both recording details of the dance recital in high definition for the documentary thereafter. The one that was to be extensively promoted on YouTube and Facebook.

The third camera, the pièce de résistance, a remote-controlled drone that had been brought from the US to get the aerial shots, had crashed perilously close to the heroine during rehearsals and gone up in flames, we were told.

In the far right corner of the stage, a bent, defeated, decrepit man clutched his heart with one hand and the curtain with the other. It was Vishwa. His great big racking sobs were muffled by the din he had sponsored.

'You know what's next?' he said.

'Bill, I think,' I said, preparing to make the most compassionate gesture I'd made all year – reaching for my wallet.

But Vishwa was in no mood to leave. He stopped me with one hand while his other signalled for refills. The waiter interpreted this as two each, slid the glasses noiselessly on to our table, and disappeared before Vishwa's hand could come down.

'She's corralled three other women, da,' Vishwa said, fast-tracking the fresh drink to his liver in two no-nonsense gulps. 'All the same size but varying degrees of insanity. And she wants to perform another bigger, better ballet … and this time, not just in Chennai. It's going to be a Grand Tour of Mumbai, Delhi and, for some reason, Bhopal. Bhopal, can you believe it? Hasn't that place already seen enough?'

'And?' I said.

'She is talking to A.R. Rahman now,' he said. 'She wants him to compose the score.'

'Oh,' I said.

'What the hell do you mean, "Oh"?' he said. 'What if the f*%$@r agrees?'

'He's supposed to be a nice chap, I hear,' I said.

'Yeah? So am I. But do you see anyone giving me half-a-mil for it? Why can't she get a mean, nasty sex offender or schizophrenic who charges less, da? Like a normal human being would?'

There was no arguing with that.

'You know, I never knew Priya was a dancer,' I said, trying to divert Vishwa.

'Are you blind? Or stupid? Or both?' he said.

I refused to be offended. He was, after all, a man who had been through so much. Plus, I'd been married for eighteen years. Vishwa hoovered another whisky and slapped the retreating rear of Bharani, our waiter. Bharani didn't object.

'Did you not *see* the performance? Did it look like dance to you? Or even a distant, mutant, stillborn cousin of dance, for that matter?' he said.

'Yes … no … a little, maybe … where did she train? In the US?' I said.

'*Train*? Train, you say? Let me tell you a story,' he said.

Let me tell you a story. How often I'd heard that line in a bar. Not once had it ended well.

'Two–three years ago,' he said, 'we were in Hawaii. Our younger one was off to college. So it was the great big family vacation preceding the empty nest. I was hanging out, doing nothing, when all of a sudden, I got chatting with this Hula dancer. You know, the grass-skirt-Hawaiian-entertainer type. Couldn't have been more than twenty-twenty-two. She wanted some advice, you know,' he said, pointing to his chest area.

'She had lung issues?' I said.

'You're a moron, da,' Vishwa said. Then with completely unnecessary hand movements, he elucidated. 'About her bazoombas, chumbawumbas, dinglebobbers, magambos, num-nums, shmozobs, splazoingas…'

I stopped him before he reached 'Z' and started from 'A' again.

'I get it. I get it. What advice?' I said.

'Fool. Listen. I was waiting for Priya to finish her waxing or yanking or some other horrific routine that fat women go through. And this girl was there. She'd danced the previous night at the resort. Total cutie, okay? I thought, what the heck, and bought her a drink and told her I was a doctor. Cancer and shit. She was impressed, I could tell. So, you know, one thing led to another, and she asked me to check her Barnes & Noble for lumps. Strictly professional, of course. Guess who walks in mid-consultation?'

'Priya, I guess,' I said.

'Ah, finally you're getting it,' he said.

'And?'

'And – that's it. Revenge saga begins. Back in Dallas, first thing our lady does is enrol herself in Bharatanatyam classes with some old leftover Kalakshetra-type chick. Kids are in college and I'm a big old lech, she says. So, apparently, the time has come for her to make a mark … and *find* herself. She's the size of a Sherman Tank, for God's sake, what's not to find?'

'Oh, so that's the story,' I said, attempting to get up and make like we should leave.

'Shots, sir,' said Bharani. By now, Vishwa and he were communicating on a plane out of my reach. Because I hadn't seen or heard a requisition for a tray of shot glasses that were filled with turquoise-blue liquor and letting out flames you could toast marshmallows on.

'You wish,' said Vishwa Sattiraju – once rumoured to be in the running for Surgeon General – swallowing a blue fireball.

He burped smoke and continued.

'After a month of very expensive classes, the old dancer guru chick, good woman that she was, asked Priya to quit. In fact, her exact words were, "Nothing in the *Natyashastra*, or *The Art of War*, for that matter, can explain what you are doing, ma." After which she moved to an undisclosed location.'

'Ah, that explains it,' I said.

'That explains nothing,' said Vishwa. He poured the contents of a shot glass over his chicken tikka and tried to light it. Bharani materialized from nowhere and replaced the soggy tikka with a fresh plate of fried baby corn.

'There's more?' I said.

'You betcha,' Vishwa said. 'See, any normal human being would've taken that guru lady's advice, given up dance and taken up mud-wrestling or sheep-shearing, right? Not our Priya. She found another guru. This one was a Golt. Taught Kuchipudi. She was made of sterner stuff and lasted two months ... till the poor thing was hospitalized. You know why?'

I shook my head.

'Well, my delicate Shrimati, all two-hundred-and-three pounds of her, jangly anklets and all, landed on the woman's foot after a high jump-type move no one saw coming.'

'Then?' I said.

'Then, nothing. I piss my pants, settle out of court with the guru, visit her in the hospital a couple of times, promise to get her son a green card, turn around and *what do I see*?'

'What?' I said.

'Priya has found *another* guru.'

'A third one?' I said.

'Yes, my friend,' he said. 'A third one ... this one was a Mallu with an unpronounceable name that taught Mohiniattam.'

'How long did that last?' I said. 'Three months?'

'You know,' my friend said, 'I can understand why your books are not selling.'

'Who told you that? Is it my editor? Don't believe her...'

'That's not the point,' he said.

We had a companion now at our table. It was Bharani. It was just the three of us left in the bar. 'The point is, any good story is always unpredictable, right, Bernie Boy?'

Bernie Boy nodded. He had already received more than his monthly salary as tips from Vishwa. He would've nodded if my wrists were being slit.

'One guru leaves, second guru leaves. If the third guru does the same thing, what kind of story arc is that?' Vishwa was addressing Bharani.

'You're right, sir,' said Bharani. 'Screenplay should always have twists. Otherwise, second half will have a lag.'

Vishwa got up. 'Home?' I said.

'Home, yes. But not yours,' said Vishwa.

Vishwa and Bharani exchanged a long and not entirely appropriate look. Then they exploded laughing.

—∾—

The tiny apartment was neat if you ignored the clothesline of multicoloured underwear bisecting the living-cum-dining-cum-bedroom. Vishwa and I sat side by side on Bharani's camp-cot. The unoccupied bits of the TV table housed our drinks. If the spatter and aroma of whatever Bernie (as he insisted on being called) was making for his new best friend were anything to go by, our one-hour journey in an auto, with Vishwa insisting on riding alongside the driver, would be worth it.

Vishwa took a long swig of the Aristocrat whisky from the steel tumbler and followed it with a slurp of the industrial-strength mango pickle straight from the half-open plastic sachet.

'This is the life, right?' he said.

I nodded. In truth, how much of it I had left would become apparent only after I went home.

'What's the twist?' I said.

'Long story short, okay? Mallu guru and Priya collaborate and start a fusion dance school. You saw her card, no? *Nritya Canyon: Texas's Only Certified School of Bharatapudiattam.* Certifiable is more like it. The deal is, Priya runs the operation and gives the Mallu chick royalties. How do you like that? All paid for by my kickbacks to the parents?'

'If you don't get angry, can I ask you something?' I said. While a simple yes would've done, Vishwa addressed the question by reaching over and giving me a full-bodied, smoky-chicken-flavoured kiss on my lips. I managed to thwart his tongue by pursing my lips just in time.

'You're my best friend, da,' he said. 'Ask me anything.' A couple of minutes ago, he'd said and done the same thing to Bharani and I could've sworn I'd seen tongue.

Bharani, for his part, had asked for a ticket to the US and a sponsorship letter. I chose not to take it personally.

'Tell me, what *is* Bharatapudiattam?' I said.

'That's your question? Simple. It is a 25-25-25 mixture of Bharatanatyam, Kuchipudi and Mohiniattam. A fusion dance form born out of the criminally depraved mind of my wife.'

'That still leaves 25, right?' I said a tad warily. Vishwa nodded.

'That, sir, constitutes the most vital ingredient – a fine pulp of my medical degree, my earnings, my sanity and my *cojones*,' he said without irony.

'I think it's a phase,' I said. I had to say something. 'She'll get over it...'

'I don't really think so,' he said. 'Why?'

'Well, you remember the drone camera, right?'

'Yes. The one that crashed when Priya was rehearsing,' I said.

'If the gods were on my side, wouldn't it have found its target?'

I nodded.

'But let me end with this,' Vishwa said. I had never seen anyone so sober. 'I must tell you about Priya's magnum opus. The dance ballet she is planning with the three other demented divas with equally tormented husbands. Guess what it's about?'

'You tell me,' I said.

'You're familiar with mythology, I hope. Apparently, Rambha, Urvashi, Menaka and Tilottama have had it up to here, okay? They are sick of being the Item Girls of Heaven, seducing random unwashed sages and all. Well, our dance ballet, a feminist parable written and directed by Ms Priya Sattiraju, with music by A.R. Rahman or Ennio Morricone if he's available, starring the Fat Wives Club of Western friggin' USA, involves the vanquishing of Lord Indra by the apsaras and a hostile takeover of Swargaloka.'

'What's it called?' I said.

'*Heaven Forbid*,' said Vishwa.

'Refill?' said Bharani.

रिश्तों की डगर है मुश्किल

प्रसून जोशी

रिश्तों की डगर है मुश्किल
ऐसे न मिलेगी मंज़िल
चलना तू संभल संभल के...

डोर ऐसी जोड़ना जो गाँठ मन की खोले
एक ऐसा रिश्ता जो मन का कोना छू ले
कांच सा नाज़ुक नहीं, शीशे जैसा साफ़...

रिश्तों की डगर है मुश्किल
ऐसे न मिलेगी मंजिल
चलना तू संभल संभल के...

रिश्ता जो चाहे रूठ जाये
पर मनाने आये
आँखों में हो सीलन मगर

Rishton Ki Dagar Hai Mushkil

Prasoon Joshi

The route to lasting ties isn't fair
It isn't easy getting there
Watch your step

Weave the threads with an art
That undoes the knots of your heart
Ties that tug at heartstrings in some part

Like glass – not fragile, but clear

Though upsets it may see,
A true relationship comes around
Even if eyes are damp, all the while

मुस्कुराने आये
पत्तों सा न उड़ जाये
शामों सा न ढल जाये
बुझते हुए रास्तों पे
उम्मीद सा जल जाये
फूल सा मुरझाये ना
खुशबू की हो बात

रिश्ता वो जिसमें दूरियाँ हों
साँस आये, जाये
तेरा भी अपना कोई गीत हो, वो भी कोई गीत गाये।
खुद तो मिटाना न चाहे
तुझको बदलना न चाहे
जैसा भी है तू तुझको
वैसे ही जो अपनाये
हो न अँधियारा घना
रात का हो ख़्वाब...

It links closer with a smile.
That, like a leaf in the wind, won't be blown away
That, like the evening sun, won't set at end of day
That like hope lights up a gloomy way
Like a flower, fragrant, never wilting away.

A relationship allows space
And lets you breathe at your pace
Where you sing your own song,
and listen too to another, all along
No desire to erase the self for your sake
Or fit you to suit another space
But gather you in all your completeness
In acceptance.
Like the night, not dark, but dreamy.

Keep Searching, a Light Might Appear

Noor Zaheer

'Dark is the night,
no light to guide
Walk I must
To keep hope alive.'

—From 'The Breeze' by Hila Sedighi, who was arrested on 7 January 2016

Let me begin at the beginning. No, not from where science says is the beginning, the Big Bang, or from the single-celled amoeba. Let us open some religious scriptures, the monotheistic ones beginning with Abraham and spreading practically all over the world. The beginning of human beings can be traced to Eve, well Adam first, and Eve a bit later when Adam gets lonely and wants a companion, because God, the typical patriarchal father, is busy with other things. With

Eve and the heavenly sanction that they are meant for each other, which religion projects as the first 'marriage', came the catch: the apple! Go anywhere, do whatever, but do not eat the forbidden fruit. Now this was unfair to Eve. She was created later; she did not know much about paradise, and in the Garden of Eden, there wasn't anything to do except listen to boring music by lute-playing houris.

Where was one to go? One valley was much like the other, as were the waterfalls, hills and flowers. And she had a mind of her own. She was unable to suppress her curiosity and her desire to explore. God had not explained what would happen if the apple was consumed. She would have been an absolute imbecile if she had not yearned to find out what would happen if she ate it. Explorer that she is, the 'woman' has always been unable to suppress her curiosity. The deprivation of Eden opened the doors of the earth for her; more space, more possibility of change and more desire to be; and more unanswered questions... So while Adam wept, repented and apologized, Eve went about making the earth habitable.

The first marriage may have been made in the heavens, but it soon became a way of life on earth as well, with sociologists claiming that public acceptance of partners with public mating was a signal of announcing mutual belonging or 'hands off' for everyone else. It was also binding on both partners. The right to choice was very much in force and later societies allowed it to exist in the forms of 'gandharva vivah' in India, '*teknopoioia*' or child bearing of the ancient Greeks, or '*hemet*'-taking (wife-taking) in ancient Egyptians.

Yet the most important concern of today is how to get out of a marriage. Social stigma, a slack judicial system, the anti-women attitude of the law enforcers and problems of taking care of children notwithstanding – there are more women who are voicing their desire to walk out of marriage than ever before. In its initial state, marriage must have allowed equal rights in choice to both partners. But, with the slow but definite growth of patriarchy, the same rights have been confiscated. The dominance of patriarchy became so strong with time, and has continued for so long, that women too have accepted it as a way of life. So deep-rooted is patriarchy and so persistent its grip on the psyche of women that it can be found manifesting itself even in rebellions like inter-caste and cross-community marriages. It is always the woman who converts, learns the language. Women even use abuses that degrade womanhood.

Having lived and worked in the Kinnaur and Lahaul Spiti districts of Himachal Pradesh, researching oral traditions and the absorption of Buddhism by the tribal communities, I realized the huge difference in the urban middle class perception of divorce and the concept as it exists in the tribal communities of this region. While in the urban set-up it is a breaking of a relationship, among the tribes it is merely a parting of paths while the road and the direction of both individuals remain the same. Upper Kinnaur practises perhaps the easiest and quickest forms of divorce. The village head and elders of the two families sit on a higher hillside. The couple walks up to them holding a stick from the '*shuk*' tree between them. This tree is considered very auspicious; its wood gives a pleasant smell when burnt and is used for making the begging bowls of Buddhist monks. On reaching the elders, the husband and wife together break the piece of wood and walk away in different directions. They are now considered divorced. They are free to either marry again, become monks or nuns, or continue their lives alone. The children move freely from one parent to the other; the now divorced couple help each other, on their land, in reconstructing their house, and participate in family weddings and social events.

But with economic reforms and development, urban respectability is nibbling into tradition, and patriarchy is beginning to find footholds. Boys and girls are now ashamed to admit that divorce is so easy in their way of life and embarrassed by the laughter this simplicity and ease generates. This feeling of mortification, of considering oneself inferior, backward or unmanly, is one of the pillars of patriarchy and reminds one of the manner in which *khula* or the woman's right to ask for a divorce was confiscated by Muslim men in the late nineteenth century.

Khula, as sanctioned in the Quran in keeping with the Arab tribal tradition, gives a woman the right to demand and get a divorce. Just as a man is to repeat talaq thrice and divorce his wife, so could a woman in the Arab tribes. Islam added a consideration period of forty days between each uttering of talaq and a waiting period of three months and ten days for a woman after the talaq to establish the fatherhood of a child conceived just before talaq was finalized.

After the first struggle for independence and the consequent defeat of the Indian forces in 1857, India was brought under the British Imperial control and made a colony; the new rulers wished to establish a judicial system that would include and assimilate the personal laws of the various religious communities residing in the subcontinent. Christianity had still not quite accepted the concept of divorce, though it had been initiated a couple of centuries back in the United Kingdom. The new rulers invited scholars from all the religions for a dialogue. Of course, all these scholars were men, even though United Kingdom had a woman, Queen Victoria, as its monarch. The Hindu scholars ruled out divorce citing the belief of the continuity of marriage through many births. The Muslim scholars maintained that men had the right to divorce their wives but were too embarrassed to uphold the right of women to do the same.

The result of having no female assertion at the time of the formulation of the first Muslim Marriage Act is that, in its present form, despite a democratic system, it manifests itself as completely binding on the woman. Innumerable women have to undergo mental and emotional traumas. Muneeza's story is an example of how Muslim women fare even today, in the twenty-first century.

Faced with the threat of talaq, Muneeza tried harder to please her husband. She offered to give up her much-loved job if that were a concern for him. She even tried to find out in discreet ways if his interest lay somewhere else, and if the cause for his random utterances of talaq were another woman. She drew a blank everywhere. He earned well; the house belonged to them, their children attended good schools. Yet, at the drop of a hat, Imtiaz would utter the first talaq and her life would turn upside down for the next month. She could not refuse to accept talaq if it came. That was not an option provided by the Holy Quran. If a man pronounced talaq the woman just had to accept it; she had no right to question or ask the reason for the divorce. He may then pronounce the talaq again after forty days and then a third and make it final; or he could stop after the first or the second, let the stipulated period lapse and allow the talaq to become invalid. So a man could, in the Shia community of Muslims, say talaq the first two times as many times as he wished. In other words, it was a whip that controlled his wife, and kept her in utter subjugation.

It took Muneeza nine years to realize that she could not go on like this. She knew she would either have a nervous breakdown, or be driven to suicide. She just had to bring this uncertain, inconsistent existence to an end. Did she or did she not belong? How long could one be expected to live in an unpredictable and unreliable relationship? She knew it would be a let-down for her in-laws, who were trying their best to make the marriage work. But she just couldn't go on. It took her a year, but she finally arrived at a decision. She was going to ask for khula – calmly, without giving vent to anger or emotional outbursts.

Anger and emotion, outbursts and humiliation came anyway, when she had learnt how difficult it was to make a khula happen.

Muneeza was asked to give reasons for wanting khula. She was questioned if she had discussed this with her husband. Was he willing to give her khula? What was the amount of compensation that had been fixed and who were the mediators? How could it be assured that the mediators did not have a vested interest? What did she plan to do after she got the khula? What was going to happen to the children? And the questioning and counter-questioning went on and on. Her explanation that she did not wish to live a life where the 'divorce' hung like a sword over her head was taken as un-Islamic, since giving talaq was a man's right. She was also told that she should be grateful that she belonged to a sect that did not allow triple talaq, and that things never came to a head and her husband did not pronounce the third and final talaq – meaning that he loved her. And so she must feel remorseful for even having thought of khula.

The advice and fatwas carried on, as her demand was tossed back and forth between her, the Shia school of jurisprudence, and the Muslim Personal Law Board.

This state of affairs persisted despite the fact that the Quran is fair and clear about khula. 'Khul' is an Arabic term that literally means 'to take out' or 'remove'. Khula is the right of any woman in Islam to demand a divorce or get a separation from her husband. After divorce the husband is responsible for the education and maintenance of the children. The children live with the mother for seven years, after which period they can live with either parent, as decided by mutual consent.

Thus, khula is basically an understanding or agreement that is reached between a husband and wife. The husband agrees to pronounce the talaq, usually after a financial settlement. In the normal course it should simply be the dower or 'meher', if it has been paid at the time of nikah. If it has not, then the meher is waived as compensation for being set free.

The *Hadith* gives an incident supporting this: In the time of the Prophet, the wife of Thabit-ibne-Qais came to the Prophet and asked him to intervene on her behalf to obtain khula. The Prophet inquired about the terms and conditions of the nikah. He was told that an orchard had been given to her as the dower or meher at the time of marriage. The Prophet then asked her if she was willing to give back to her husband the orchard he had given her. The woman accepted this demand and got khula.

The present scenario is that there are a large number of men who adopt a vengeful attitude of deliberately torturing women who do not wish to continue the alliance. The majority of men are not willing to accept the fact that a woman is walking out of the marriage. So they put across some other demands. These demands are usually either a big sum of money or the forfeiting of her visiting rights to meet her children. In either case the woman is in a weak position. In the first case she might not have enough money to 'buy' the khula. It may be that she wishes to live off the income of the land, house, orchard that the man is now demanding. Parting with these would reduce her financial and social status. In the second case, it simply amounts to emotional blackmail, because no woman would want a divorce at the cost of cutting off all ties with her children.

Yet, if the husband accepts the terms being offered and agrees to khula, he is asked to pronounce talaq in exchange.

Thus, it is up to the woman to somehow cajole, persuade and prevail upon the husband to give her a divorce. She has to waive her dower, or part with a substantial amount of money, or sell off or gift immovable property to somehow bring the man to the point where he agrees to the parting of ways. Even after all this, it is still the man who is divorcing the woman and not the woman divorcing the man, since it is he who has to pronounce the talaq.

The very concept of divorce is based on incompatibility. If the man does not want a woman, he has the right to leave her. Why doesn't she have the same right? Why is she compelled to give socially accepted reasons, and in modern times file an anti-dowry case or police complaint? Some women have had to resort to lawlessness by hiring goons to terminate the marriage. Why?

Supposing the man is adamant about not pronouncing talaq and insists on a compensation that he knows is beyond the woman's means to pay, while on the other hand the woman is equally insistent upon obtaining khula – what happens then?

The *Hadith* tells us that, in such a case, a person respected in society and acceptable to both as mediator should be appointed. This person is to hear both sides, take stock of the financial status of both the parties, arrive at an amount to be paid as compensation to the husband and inform them of his decision. This decision would then be binding on both and khula would become a certainty.

In case of this arbitration, and if the woman refers her case to the Muslim Personal Law Board or to the maulvi nearby, she is immediately expected to provide reasons for her desire to separate from her husband. The maulvi consults the higher authority on behalf of the woman. The higher authority depends on the sect to which both belong as there are different schools of jurisprudence with their specific interpretations of the Quran.

According to the *Hadith*, a woman does not need to give a reason for wanting khula. An incident quoted in the *Hadith* supports this:

A lady, married for six years, came to the Prophet and asked him to intervene as she wished to obtain khula from her husband. The Prophet inquired about the reason for her wishing to dissolve the marriage. The woman kept silent. The Prophet again queried if her husband's character was questionable to which she answered that there was nothing wrong with his character as he was pious and God-fearing. He then asked if he was hot-tempered or physically abusive. The woman again replied in the negative. However, she still insisted on khula. The Prophet then did not ask that she reveal the reason and awarded khula to her.

The Prophet is later said to have explained to his followers: 'If a man divorces he must present the reason to the qazi; however, if a woman wants a khula and she is not willing to reveal the reason, the qazi must not insist [she do so] and should award her the khula.'

Thus, the Prophet takes into account that the qazi would be a man and the woman would feel awkward in revealing personal or intimate experiences that may have led her to demand khula. It also allows for a woman to seek divorce from one man because she prefers another and not to reveal this fact to anyone. The decision of the Prophet also accepts that a woman must have examined all options, perhaps also requested the elders in the family to intervene and advise both, failing which she had to request for khula.

Contrary to this, the present Muslim personal law in India absolves the man from providing any reason for divorce, yet insists that the woman give a reason that is 'acceptable' to the qazi.

In the course of my work and research, I meet and speak to many women, and some of their stories are indeed heart-rending. Zarina's story is one that illustrates the helpless position Muslim women are forced into.

'It is happening again.' It was possible that the stress of the situation made the words come out involuntarily, despite her hesitation about sharing details of her life with me.

About six years ago, Zarina's father got her married to the son of a close friend's business partner. She was about to turn seventeen at the time.

'I think he [her father] believed he was doing what was best for me,' she said. In reality, the marriage turned out to be anything but the 'best thing' for Zarina.

Knowing that she belonged to a conservative household, where all women observed strict purdah, there was no need for me to ask whether her consent was taken before the marriage was fixed. It was not. She had just been told. Zarina saw the man for the first time after her nikah, and her first reaction was one of discomfort bordering on fear.

Within six months of her marriage, Zarina's father unexpectedly passed away, turning her already verbally abusive husband into a physically violent one. He only stopped beating her when his mother told him that Zarina might be carrying a boy. Zarina put up with the torture, living in hope. 'My mother would say that I should wait for the child to be born and everything will be fine,' she said, explaining why she never remonstrated.

After the child was born the change did come. But it was for the worse. Zarina gave birth to a healthy baby boy. Her reward for that: Her husband didn't beat her for a month. But after that grace period was over, she lived through some of the darkest moments of her life, as the violence was resumed.

Everyone in the house knew; her father-in-law, mother-in-law, brother-in-law, the servants, everyone. He wouldn't hold back from beating her publicly over something like the drinking water not being the right temperature. But no one batted an eyelid.

She recalls seeing sympathy in her mother-in-law's eyes just once when her husband flung her down the stairs six months after she had given birth to their son. That fall landed Zarina in hospital with broken ribs and several fractures. Of course, everyone was told she had slipped and fallen. Zarina was too scared to dispute the story.

Somehow, her mother managed to convince her mother-in-law to let her take Zarina home after she had spent about a week in hospital. Her husband now wouldn't allow her to see her son. Eventually after two weeks, dragged back by her love for her son, Zarina returned to that hell. And it was as fiery as she had expected it to be. Sometimes before and sometimes after he beat her, he would rape her to exert his power. Zarina suffered an early miscarriage during her second pregnancy, the result of another torturous beating by her husband. After that, her brother, who was barely fifteen at the time, came over one day when her husband wasn't at home, and took her back to her mother's house.

Zarina's demands for divorce have been rejected by her husband who has married again and refuses to let Zarina meet her son. It has been four years since she has seen her little boy, but family pressure is building – she has a younger sister who is turning sixteen, and in order for her to marry, Zarina's status as a divorcee needs to change. The family is negotiating a divorce now so that, for the second time in her life, Zarina can be forced into marriage.

Today, in spite of so many marriage counsellors, women's cells and crisis centres at various police stations, women are still reluctant to open up when their marriage breaks down. Invariably they try to find a reason to defend the man's abusive nature, his drunkenness, his not helping in household chores. How many times have we heard apologetic excuses that range from 'actually his mother never loved him', or 'he is not getting his due promotion' or 'his father was like this' from abused and tortured women! Often there is the misplaced sense of pride, evident in statements like – 'he does nothing in the house'; 'he doesn't know one spice from the other'; 'he doesn't know what a kitchen is for.' One is forced to think that it is perhaps the shame a woman feels over nurturing her fear – of not hitting back and of not being able to defend herself – that paves the way for these excuses.

Maybe before we explore the role of patriarchy in divorce, we have to examine its role in finding suitable partners for girls. A girl at eighteen can exercise her right and vote to power a government of her choice. This government can make policies related to education, health, development, agriculture, etc. Hence, though selecting the government is a big responsibility – influencing the course of governance and the administration of an entire nation – women have a right to this selection. Yet in India it is still largely assumed that a young woman, even if educated and qualified, cannot select a life partner.

One should, however, not imagine that women are in a better situation where laws are flexible and customs, seemingly women-friendly, replace rigid laws. Customs and traditions can be equally restrictive when it comes to women walking out of a marriage. In the Spiti subdivision of the Lahaul Spiti district, both polyandry and abduction are common among the Swangla tribe as a means of finding wives. These customs are considered legal and binding and there exists no way for the women to fight these. A girl is married to several brothers of the same family and this is acceptable to the community which sees it as a continuation of the 'Draupadi Pratha'. Though tribal customs dictate that the girl's agreeing to the marriage is a precondition for a marriage to take place, reality proves otherwise. Often the ceremony is conducted between a girl and a family's eldest son, and as the younger siblings grow, they, in turn, become the girl's partners.

The abduction of a girl by a group of young men is frowned upon, but if they succeed in taking the girl inside one of their houses, the girl belongs to the boy of the house. There is no way a marriage can be refused and once it takes place there is no way a girl can get out of it.

Feminism had begun asserting itself in Europe in the last decades of the nineteenth century and by early twentieth century it was a proper movement that was demanding equal opportunities, the right to choice and, most important, was propagating feminist thought and perspective as a viable alternative to a patriarchal way of life. By the fifth decade of the twentieth century, its waves were reaching the Indian shore and finding many supporters in Asia. In India the seriousness of the issue and its repercussions were being examined and the need for such a movement was being accepted. Its immediate effect can be seen in women picking up their pens to write their own stories. A large portion of this writing is centred round marriage, divorce, and the right to choose. Most writing by women tell a tale of oppression and a tale of fearlessness. And that is why the female pen creates such fear in society. Freedom of expression for the woman is the liberation of the entire society, because bonds are never broken alone. Once women are no longer afraid of these boogies called rape, molestation, murder, spinsterhood – they shall win the battle against them and for the rest of humanity.

But till that happens, till the battle 'to be' is won and gender equality becomes a way of life, women have to keep facing situations that are based on ownership.

Most women in India, in spite of there being a constitution that guarantees equal rights to all the citizens of this country, have an uphill task of getting out of a relationship that is so easy to form. While discussion has begun on the right of choice – and it should rightly include simpler ways of breaking the bonds – somehow getting out is not yet being explored from the female perspective. While one admires the concept of 'a cage with an open door', that which defines 'live-in' relationships as the modern version of the gandharva vivah, one does wonder how ancient women broke free of these ties. While Dushyant could conveniently forget and end the relationship, could

Shakuntala, had the need arisen, have done the same? Of all these Indian women, the plight of the Indian Muslim woman is perhaps the worst. Fundamentalists are neither accepting the Indian constitution as binding nor are they allowing reforms within Islam.

The majority of the Muslim community fails to understand that what we are doing to our daughters in the name of tradition and customs is criminal. The Anti–Child Marriage Bill has been shot down as un-Islamic in Pakistan and demands have been made in India to lower the age of marriage for Muslim girls. Forced marriages remain dominant practices, in spite of the law, and often someone other than the reluctant bride says yes from behind the curtain at the nikah. No one checks, no one contests and, of course, if it should happen that a girl wants khula, no one stands with the girl fighting for a divorce in a marriage that never happened.

Recently, the Uniform Civil Code has been in the news again. Babasaheb Ambedkar, when questioned about Article 15, 25 and 44 on religious freedom, had said that he hoped that people would realize the benefits of a Uniform Civil Code and would voluntarily accept it. This has not happened, but any discussion on this is rejected outright and considered an effort by the majority community to 'swallow the minorities'. The result being that Muslim women continue to be the minority within the minority, walking the dark tunnel of archaic laws, interpreted and enforced by pervert clergymen, with no voice on marriage, divorce, maintenance, custodial rights, and seeing no light at the end of the tunnel.

Our Bi-continental Marriage

Kalyan Ray

All the omens of the aged NRI's presaged disaster. Almost everyone was sure, except the two of us.

'Listen, she has divorced two already,' they murmured in unison, like a Bengali version of a Greek tragedy.

'Well, that's perfect then,' I countered. 'I've been divorced twice before.'

'And she's famous, a celebrity,' they said ominously, with much head-shaking.

'That too is perfect. I too am famous within my small circle of friends. And if you argue that I am not, then, since I am a professor and generally far from the public eye, that makes it a symmetrical case of opposites attracting each other. So, we have the perfect symmetry and the perfect contrast so far.'

'You know she has two daughters from the earlier marriages?'

'Well – and so do I. And a son.'

My well-wishers shook their collective heads balefully. One particular couple decided, unilaterally, to break off all relations with me because of my decision to marry. This was odd – for they had just come back from an eighteen-month stint in South Korea, during which time they had left me with a request to take care of their house. That meant my making all the arrangements for having their landscaping, plumbing problems (a pipe froze during the winter) and snow-removal in their prolonged absence. After all, they had said soulfully, I was their friend. Now, they decided I was not. They still owe me money.

The other members of the advisement posse muttered good wishes and left, as if from a funeral.

Aparna and I had met during my (very brief) stint as a member of a Bengali cultural association in the US. It was the first and last time I ever joined such an organization which periodically threw off the stupor induced by weekend after weekend with 'goat-meat parties' and occasionally organized amateur plays and hilariously off-key, but earnest, musical evenings. The rest of the week was taken over by long evening telephone calls and ever-innovative gossip. Few backs were left unstabbed. And when any celebrities from India came within their ambit, they dressed to their teeth, encumbered by heavy gold jewellery and hurled themselves forward – an NRI cultural phalanx – to become the inner group of NRI 'friends' of that hapless visitor.

When it became clear that Aparna (who always travelled with Rita Dey, her Chinese-Indian hairdresser and friend) was not at all interested in fluffy fan chatter and endless banal chit-chat, the organizers were hard put to find someone to undertake the onerous job of driving her from city to city. And since this was the time for the summer break, and I had lots of vacation time, I was drafted.

It was during these long drives that we got to know each other better. Earlier, at a party when Aparna escaped the clutches of fans and their mindless chatter – she had spent the evening away from the crowd, sitting by the swimming pool – when we discovered our deep interest in the Irish poet W.B. Yeats (her favourite poet and mine) and Jibanananda Das – whose poems I had translated. She recited her father Chidananda Dasgupta's translations of the same poems of Das. She can recite yards of poetry, and I realized that I had never met anyone who was so much fun to be with!

A week later, shortly before she was to return to India, I suggested a short visit to Harper's Ferry – a place in West Virginia where two rocky rivers, the Shenandoah and the Potomac, meet. It is a beautiful spot – and she had spoken of her love for rugged greenery amid rocks and mountain streams; she used to own a place like this in McCluskieganj in present-day Jharkhand.

In her usual direct manner, she turned to me and said, 'I am not interested in an affair.'

'I was going to propose marriage,' I told her, equally directly.

In complete panic, she rushed off to the nearest phone booth (this was long before the era of cellphones) and, emptying all her coins into her palm, she called her elder daughter. I found this completely disarming. It was only over the years that I found out that Aparna always consults her kitchen cabinet (her father, when he had been still with us, and both her daughters) before she makes any really serious decision.

We decided, after receiving the blessings of her daughters – Konkona was twelve – and the somewhat puzzled acquiescence of her parents, that we would marry. Well, that was that.

So we did, at a brief civil ceremony in the tiny village of Mansfield. It was conducted by the deputy mayor, a farmer, who took time off his tractor, tilling his field. With the two witnesses – two Greco-American friends – we had a lovely post-wedding lunch at the Italian restaurant in the village, starting with exquisite eggplant rollatini and a fine chilled white wine from Ravello. My Indian friends stayed away. Actually, I did not even consider inviting them.

When we returned to my tiny apartment filled with books, art objects, my collection of masks from various countries on the walls, more books, and a mattress on the floor, Aparna began our new life together by first organizing the kitchen.

In a week, we flew to India to meet all my new relatives.

Since that time, our bi-continental marriage has involved many more flights. I continued to teach in the US, and she directed her films in India, acted occasionally, and edited highly successful women's magazines – which most men also read. In that first year, when international calls were quite expensive, I had managed to notch up phone bills that were larger than the rent I paid for my apartment!

But I now realize in retrospect that we had also begun to do something that was almost unique in modern marriages. We wrote letters.

We wrote on fine lightweight letter paper, with fountain pens, in elegant envelopes, and also on the backs of whatever sheets of paper we could lay our hands on when we felt the urge to tell each other something – something we did constantly. I have all her letters from that first year, all 197 of them, for she wrote me every other day or so, sometimes more frequently. Multi-page letters, about ourselves, what we were doing, thinking, reading, dreaming, and all the other things that made up our daily lives of the mind. I went to India twice a year – in the summer for a long vacation, and in the winter for about six weeks. So the letters were like journals for each other, and somehow, also for ourselves.

And then, as if by technological serendipity, phone calls to India became cheaper – and then ridiculously cheap. And now we speak to each other, not just every day, but sometimes multiple times a day.

But I really think that those letters – written almost every day in our first year together, when we communed with each other, about ourselves, our sense of the world and art, the events that surrounded us, society, politics, poems recently read, plays seen, the many films we watched on two separate continents – created for us a space which few new marriages find to build on. Our letters, I think in retrospect, were like gardens – private gardens of many leaves, many branches, many paths that we jointly made and explored and shared.

When we are gone, we have told our daughters, it might be an interesting thing for lovers in the future to read the letters, and see how our love connected, and grew, and matured during that one year in the early '90s of the last century. I think I would want to read these letters, if I were not myself. But I do not want to change places with anyone!

But the reality is that for more than half the year – for all these years – we have lived on two separate continents; we have had two homes. We referred to them as 'our' home in Kolkata, and 'our' home in America.

At first, our home in America was my small 'ex-bachelor' apartment overlooking a green hillock, not far from the Delaware River, next to Pennsylvania. I wanted Aparna to return and spend some time each year here in America, bringing Konkona and her own parents with her. I wanted the whole family here, and have real family time together – and early summer is a magical time in this part of the world!

So I took Aparna with me to a good number of sites to look at houses, some older ones, some under construction, and some that existed yet on the builders' blueprints. It was while we were returning to our apartment that we saw in the slanted light of one afternoon ('magic hour' in film-maker's parlance) a house being constructed on a hillside with a sweeping view of the valley beneath and dense woods beside it, on a steep decline of an adjacent hill.

'That,' she said pointing, 'is a good place.'

And so we went there, and finding the floor plan good and the views breathtaking, we decided on it. This was our place on Overlook Drive, in the hill's cul-de-sac. This area was called 'The Hills of Independence', where in subsequent years – it took eight months to complete the building – we would spend a good part of late spring and early summer. Konkona decorated her bedroom, and especially her bathroom, as she pleased, and Aparna decorated the rest of the house. I did not even want to buy a spoon or spatula for the kitchen until she came and we could do all this together. Putting that home together – where we lived together and separately for twenty years – was more than just that. It defined our chosen life together, and remains full of memories of her parents, our first grandchildren, our lives intertwining.

Then there were our homes in Kolkata: first Alipur, and when we needed more space, the penthouse in Bengal Silver Spring with its lovely terrace on which we had put old dwarf bougainvillea trees which bloomed around the year. But the America house was precious, for it was a space where Aparna was always in a holiday mood. We ate late lazy breakfasts, lunch on the deck under the huge colourful umbrella, the table replete with fresh breads, salads and chinaware we had picked up from Mexico, and the sparkle of light caught in goblets of chianti wine. The hawks wheeled high above the treetops of the sleepy hillside. These were precious times, although the weeks sped by, too quickly indeed.

But we made temporary homes wherever we could, Aparna and I, in other far-flung parts of the world where our work – or whim – took us. Soon after our marriage, one mid-summer, I went off to the Philippines with my new bride in tow, to teach a seminar funded by the Luce Foundation. We were to stay the whole time in a hotel, but the day we reached, Aparna called the manager and completely transformed our suite, bringing in writing desks, replacing chairs, re-hanging curtains, replacing lamps until I escaped and came back to a space, completely transformed – for the entire duration of our stay. Even when we departed for trips to the hills of Baguio and other places in the islands, the manager loyally and cheerfully kept our suite exactly as Aparna wanted it.

We made similar 'homes' for ourselves when we took trips to various parts of Mexico. Our clear favourite was Oaxaca – although a lovely old hotel in Mexico City is possibly a close second. But then, we also have very fond memories of the little boutique in Buenos Aires hotel in Argentina, the odd high windows in our room off the Santa Maria della Novella church in the heart of Florence, or the strangely luxurious tents in the game parks of Kenya. In all these far places, Aparna would re-arrange things and create a space for us with her unique signature.

But now, we are at the threshold of something that is going to be completely new for both of us. Yet it is that very thing that is taken for granted by almost all couples of the world. From next May, I shall wind up my forty-plus-year sojourn in America, and return permanently to India. 'Coming full circle,' I keep saying to myself! And for the first time in our lives, Aparna and I shall be living together, husband and wife, round the year.

It will, then, be the twenty-third year of our bi-continental marriage.

The Imperfect Marriage

HARIMOHAN PARUVU

We are an odd couple. Odder than most. I stand six feet two inches tall, or somewhere in that region. Shobha avers I am an inch shorter. Shobhs is an inch shy of five feet or somewhere thereabouts. I feel she is many inches taller.

The gap of fifteen inches, give or take some, is wider than one can imagine. For those who think it's not much, these fifteen inches are equivalent to the distance between Earth and the planet where aliens live. This gap has catapulted us into an orbit beyond convention, social acceptability, conformity and plain normal.

There are some other minor differences. I am dark, tentative, gruff and distant. Shobhs is fair, articulate and affectionate. I am the last-bencher, sports (duh), casual type. Shobhs is the first-bencher, gold medallist and world-is-set-for-you types. I am sullen. She is witty. I mumble. She is clear as a bell. I eat. She cooks. I drive. She shops. I am Telugu. She is Maharashtrian. Together we are as different as pesarattu and poha. Why we got drawn to one another like moths to a flame is something that makes no sense, to most. Me included.

Going against the norm

Ever since we met in college two decades ago, and chose to spend more time than required with each other, the difference in our vertical dispositions attracted the attention of many. There seemed to be an unstated law that fat and thin, tall and short, fair and dark, and their combinations thereof, were not ideal for couples. To be honest, we were not thinking of marriage then, so fifteen inches or thirty inches did not matter to us. All that mattered then was to be with the person who was most fun. Many movies, common friends, ping-pong, music, exams, parties, and ups and downs later, we were still together, while others had dropped off. When she went home to Pune after collecting her gold medal, I got a job in Pune too. After another year together, we thought we should continue the good work on a long-term basis. We decided to marry, before people asked uncomfortable questions. The height issue was a non-issue. We got married. The questions never came.

After marriage, I gained a new ability. I could see people thinking when they saw us – 'How funny', and then, 'Why did they not find someone closer to their height?' A fifteen-inch difference in height is fine between friends, but not partners. No one said it out loud, except my mom – may her outspoken soul rest in peace – but I can see these thoughts, clear as a ticker tape on a TV monitor. Their eyes go to the top of my head and then to Shobha's, at times to other body parts, as they mentally calculate several things at the same time and then think 'Wow'. Then their thoughts gush out in a disorganized fashion. What's wrong with these people? They must have been doped when they got married. What losers. How desperate. A fifteen-inch gap can disrupt peace like nothing else.

Clearly the popular idea of a good marriage is to find someone close to your height, your colour, your race, your whatever, so you look pleasant together, like models in an advertisement. You do not marry and mess with other people's heads. Why would anyone do that?

Here's the big answer. I don't know. I cannot pin down any reason why we got married when we knew full well that fifteen inches separated our two worlds. Especially, when there were many reasons not to.

For starters, the pointed attention we drew from curious members of the public was an unsettling experience. Since we're not the celebrity type, we baulked at being stared at as if we had just gotten off from an alien spaceship in silver suits and beeping antennae. You see, being stared at can deter most people from a lifetime commitment – to being stared at. So many broke off with a cheery 'it was good while it lasted, but see you in the next lifetime when we have matching heights, darling'. But we said nothing of that sort, especially the darling bit, and kept going. Our four-year courtship gave us enough practice of being stared at, and enough time to reconsider and return to our separate worlds. Awkward moments, jokes about Amitabh and Jaya, some embarrassed laughs; but we stayed. The story continued. Our lives are going on okay. Imperfectly, but chugging along.

But why, ask the perfectionists. Why not, I counter. One needs answers.

Perfect versus imperfect marriages

The sacred institution of marriage must conform to acceptable norms, say the perfectionists. A difference of six inches to eight is okay, but fifteen is way too much. One must be normal. Acceptable.

I do not agree. All I know is that fifteen inches is not much of a distance. It's not like we need a megaphone to communicate or take a train to meet one another across the gap. Even considering that, the distance is greater than 'normal' – didn't someone say that distance makes the heart grow fonder? In that case, wider gaps should be recommended to increase fondness in marriages. Unless, fondness is not considered a useful attribute in marriage, of course. (As a case in point, I know a lot of couples with no gaps, whose hearts have no fondness for one another any more.)

Some feel that we may have prematurely leapt into our mismatched matrimony in a state of panic because we did not meet anyone closer to our elevation. It's not so. We did meet people closer to our eye level. I met taller girls – some only slightly taller than Shobhs – but for some reason they behaved like they were some twenty feet taller. The only advantage I could conceive with girls of the prescribed height was that when I reached out, I found a waist to slide my hand around. Now, I place my hand on Shobha's shoulder in an avuncular manner. If I insist on the waist, I'd develop orthopaedic problems of a permanent nature. Sliding hands around waists is a fine sport, but how much time do we spend on that activity? My statistics show that it is less than 1 per cent of total time spent with spouse. Other chores in a marriage do not have much to do with compatible heights either (including what's on your mind, pal). In fact, surprisingly few married jobs require physical contact after the first couple of years, unless you wish otherwise. And, theoretically, one can always slide hands around friendly, responsive waists if one misses the waist action so much.

On her part, Shobhs, I am sure, must have had an excellent selection of natty, dapper and decent boys to choose from, instead of the *junglee*, King Kong ones like me (beauty and the beast was another title given to us). She could have chosen a life that was similar to the one her many fair friends had chosen – with *chikna* husbands, secure jobs, well-furnished homes, perfect family pictures in exotic vacations, etc. But for some reason, best known to her, she chose to hang out with me and watch, mostly with growing horror, my suicidal ways of finding the toughest thing to do in the world, like a lemming on a mission to jump off a cliff. And, she is still around.

All of the above evidence goes to prove that we chose each other willingly and with a sane mind. There was no force, no shotguns, no unplanned developments from our companionship that led to the marriage. If there is one thing we could be guilty of, it's that we were too lazy to look around in the marriage supermarket. We picked the first one that fit (or did not) and threw it in the bag. It's still around. Happens with everyone right? What's the big deal?

It's a big deal to a world that wants perfection and order. The world suffers at our constant reminder of imperfection and imbalance. It cannot tolerate the mismatch. It wants to understand why the tall junglee chose petite pretty. And why petite pretty chose tall junglee. Some wiring defect?

They whisper to one another. This behaviour indicates a smallness in the tall one's thinking. Perhaps there is an inherent insecurity he is subliminally addressing by choosing petite. Or is it indicative of a bigness in her thought. Maybe she exerts a mysterious control over large, insecure bodies from her small frame. Some feel that he has lost ground by giving away precious inches he has earned genetically. Others think she is a winner because she has now added to her genetic pool. Frankly, we never thought about it because we did not understand the subconscious or genetics.

Some opine that we were rebelling against the world and our parents. Why else would she not wear high heels and reduce the offensive gap? And why does he not wear low heels, true to his nature? Far as I know, Shobhs never liked high heels, and never will. She will wear the flattest footwear one can find in the world. And I am still looking for lower heels than me of course. Rebellion is far from our lives. We don't have any causes, save saving ourselves. I don't think Shobhs adopted me to prove something to her world, nor was I trying to prove anything to the six-footer club. If there was one crime we committed, it was that we did not bother to impress the rest of the world. I was not parading a trophy wife so everyone could stand up and go 'Awww'. Nor was Shobhs looking to please her family with a decent boy with pension benefits, ESOPs and a villa on one of the foreign coasts. Our families appeared to be happy that we were getting married and moving on. To whom, it did not matter really.

They ask, maybe, some masochistic streak exists in both? Yes. But that's true of most couples, is it not, we counter. Then they ask, could you have married for love? I find that difficult to answer because we don't behave like lovers. We, at best, hang out together in our lives. We do not fall over each other, nor do mad passions rule our world. Only time will tell, when we have that moment of clarity, hopefully by the end of this essay, if it was love or not. But as of now, life's flowing by and we're still with, and at, one another, on a daily basis.

Mental compatibility versus physical incompatibility

Our compatibility seems to belong to a mental space and not the physical world. In our mental universe, my mental arm is comfortably placed around her mental waist most of the time, i.e., we are perfectly compatible. It's good enough for me. I feel there is a case for mental compatibility to be a bigger factor than physical compatibility for marriages. When I look at 'perfect' couples I wonder: 'Is life in their matching-heights paradise better? The same bitter fights take place even there. What's the big deal in this perfect-height business then?'

Perfection, it appears, is not as perfect as it is made out to be.

On the other hand, I feel, imperfect is the real perfect. There is no strain on anyone. We are imperfect by choice. She can wear her flattest sandals and I can hide my head in the clouds. We do our own things: share fears and apprehensions, tears and laughter. We still do the things we did in college – watch movies, read books, watch tennis and cricket matches, ignore politics, be broke.

Life is good. Life is imperfect. It's not a bad thing. We're still alive.

Dealing with the physical world

However blissful our mental world is, we cannot avoid the tyranny of the physical world we live in. To deal with it, we've devised our own ingenious methods. Over time, we have figured out how to manoeuvre ourselves so we appear less odd together. A slight distance between us when we walk creates an optical illusion, and makes the fifteen inches appear like a more acceptable eight inches. This requires one of us to get a head start while the other delays the proceedings a bit, so it's a matter of timing, really. We have perfected a way to stand when together, which creates some superb inch-dissipating frames. We slip and slide into postures and balance photographs by a shift of leg, hip or neck. We have devised many such devices to muffle the dissonance. Even people around us move intuitively to lower the fifteen-inch gap.

These manoeuvres work well among civilized people, i.e., people who don't stare too obviously or laugh too loudly in our faces (ha, they can only laugh at one face at a time!). The problem is with the uncivilized lot, who stare at us as if they are waiting for an explanation. They stand by as if we are an unfinished act that forgot to end. What next? Why? They don't know that this is the final act, that there are no further answers.

With this crowd we avoid eye contact lest they ask for selfies. Then there are less intimidating types who stare surreptitiously and smile to themselves. We promptly intimidate and out-stare them. If being stared at is inevitable, we enjoy it and smile.

Shobhs tells me that she has trouble talking to me when we stand close to one another. I always suspected she looks up to me and this confirmation warms my heart. At the same time, she is convinced that I look down upon her. I cannot refute her allegation because she has documentary evidence. Her neck hurts. My back hurts. These are small sacrifices we have to make to stay together.

Or apart, in our case.

Advantages and disadvantages of imperfect marriages

Is it worth going through all this trouble, some wonder. What's the purpose of all this, they ask.

Of course it is worth it.

Imperfections bring several unseen advantages. As a team, we reach out to different levels and altitudes at home, which hand us a huge competitive advantage over our rival, same-height couples. Our domestic work is well distributed. We address our respective latitudes and longitudes with complete ownership and zero interference. There is no gender bias; I get the ceiling, she the floor. We give each other lots of space. I can't poke my nose into her space without troubling my lower back and she can't poke into mine without troubling her neck.

Mismatched marriages last longer because we communicate at different levels. No one hears what the other is saying unless we are sitting face to face, which is rare. Many things go unnoticed – like the faces we make at one another – because our faces have slightly distant coordinates. (In normal marriages people have to make faces behind their spouse's back.) Consequently, I have not heard of any couple from our mismatched tribe, our ambassadors Amitabh and Jaya included, who has separated despite temptations calling at their respective heights. Compare this with several 'height-perfect' couples we know, and I rest my case. Was it the quest for perfection that did them in? Have we been saved by our acceptance of imperfection? Food for thought surely.

Another benefit is that we are constantly on our toes. We bump into new people and new reactions. Some are frightfully original – 'Arre Amitabh and Jaya'. Some behave as if one of us is not in the room depending on whom the person knows. Most people deal with only one of us at a time. If they try to address both of us they normally end up with a pain in the neck.

There are times when we meet each other by chance too. If I sit down on the stool suddenly, or she stands on a table, it makes for a delightful, surprise meeting. We see each other and note how we have changed since last time. (Most other times she is talking to my midriff while I deal with the space over the top of her head.) All in all, it is a meditative, being-present kind of awareness. Life is interesting.

There are other happy side effects. We make people happy. One moment people in the hall are looking like they could burst into tears, out of boredom, and the next moment their eyes light up when they see us. Fat aunty stares. She nudges the emaciated giraffe next to her. A new energy spreads in the room. For a while people forget their marriages, spouses, debt, ugliness, poverty, bad habits, choices, sad lives and all other troubles. We are like religion, drugs or movies – on a smaller scale. There cannot be a nobler purpose to our marriage.

We believe we contribute to the general health of society. If ordinary people see perfect couples – like say, Angelina Jolie and Brad Pitt – they tend to burn with jealousy and resentment, and lose their self-esteem, which affects their health negatively. In such a scenario we are better than Jolie and Pitt. People feel secure when they are around us. Also, we are making society equal in our own way by balancing the average height of the world.

There are far too many nice things associated with our marriage. I feel like we deserve an award.

There are some disadvantages. On the physical front, as mentioned earlier, walking around arm in arm in Puducherry might not happen because of the prospect of strained backs and necks. Car seats need to be pushed fully back or fully forward depending on who is driving. Car models have to be chosen carefully. Same with furniture and fittings. Too high, and she will need a leg up. Too low and I will need the services of a crane to extricate myself. On the psychological side, we sometimes feel lonely because the other person is in his own or her own level. It's like we are living in two different stories. But net-net, as they say these days, there are no big complaints.

The final argument

The hardliners do not buy this. They say it is a case of sour grapes. That I am making it sound like I am better off, when I am not. Here's the citric acid test then. The only way to look at it is this – is the marriage in working condition and does it still have some juice left? From all indications, it looks like it does, on both counts. It's running well after twenty years, in a lopsided manner admittedly, like Basanti's tonga – God bless Basanti and Dhanno and the tonga (should have been Amitabh and Jaya in that scene!) – outrunning the villains.

I believe that there could be a higher purpose to this imperfect affair. That in accepting each other fully as we, Shobhs and I, are perhaps learning what we most need to learn, to accept our extreme sides, the other sides. Me, my smallness. She, her tallness. And so on. We are rounding off our edges, and making the unit whole and together. I can see that my arrogance and overconfidence have been reduced to manageable levels and Shobha's insecurities are lesser. I can see how it is perfect, how we first make peace with one another, and our differences, and then integrate the other extreme. Two inches, ten inches, twenty inches – inside we are all the same, with the same fears and apprehensions.

These days Shobha appears taller than me in many aspects with her clarity and courage. I have learnt to step back in areas where I am no good and let her steer those issues. We know that what drew us together was the respect we had for each other as individuals. One cannot compromise this respect. It's life, and it has to be respected.

The signs are good. The distances between us are narrowing as we walk. People who stare have stopped bothering us. We are more comfortable as a couple, and as we get more comfortable, the inches seem to disappear. When I look back, I cannot think of getting married to anyone else but Shobhs. Fifteen inches or twenty inches, it would have been Shobhs. The fifteen inches are perfect. A few inches here and there, and we would not have tuned into that mysterious frequency that brought us together. In some lopsided way it must be love, that frequency, hidden among those missing inches.

And that, my dear readers, is the long and short of an imperfect couple's marriage.

Marriage and Me

Deeksha Nagar

When I think of marriage, the winding lanes of Chowk in old Lucknow open like pages of a graphic novel before me. A novel I could read before I knew how to read. A novel full of enigmatic characters, with knotty relationships, who snarled unforgettable words and expressions of love and rage. As a child, I could look at those words but could not grasp their underlying meanings. Like all children, I repeated, narrated and re-enacted what I saw. I accepted the stories around me unquestioningly. The complex web of relationships cast within those narrow lanes of Chowk framed my notions of the lives of the married and the unmarried.

Within the walls of the dilapidated mansion we resided in, I witnessed the lives of several couples and one bachelor simultaneously. I saw the tussle between my grandparents, who had been married for over fifty years; my artist uncle and his quiet wife who communicated with each other in monosyllables; my scientist father who lulled my tired mother to sleep with his monologues full of ambitious projects. Then there was a second family of an elderly village woman named Amrai Devi.

Amrai Devi had come to work for my grandparents in early 1960s and, over the years, her children and grandchildren had become part of our everyday life. She had two children from her first husband and when he passed away she was 'made to sit' with another man, for in her community a woman could be married only once. She had three more children from her second union. Amrai Devi had moved in with our family upon the death of her 'second man'. Amrai Devi, with her married children and grandchildren, brought a strong village connection to the nature of marital relationships in our lives. Among this houseful of people lived a confirmed bachelor, whom we called Baba. His name was Sanchit Singh and he had run away from his village in eastern Uttar Pradesh at the age of twelve or thirteen. He had been with our family since 1938, when my father was still a baby.

Baba had chosen not to marry. When anyone asked him why he didn't marry, he would say, 'Many people tried to find someone suitable for me, and I was tempted. But then I thought marriage is just a trap. I left my home to escape from the *moha maya* and marriage would encase me again within the very walls I tried to escape. I don't want to be bound again in such a web of relationships. I will not marry.'

When I looked outside my house, I saw a neighbourhood full of buas, chachas, bhaiyyas and didis. They were not blood relations, but if they called my father bhaisahab (brother) they were my chachas (uncle). If they sought my grandmother's advice like a daughter or a granddaughter, they were my aunt or sister. My neighbours were my extended family.

To an outsider, the narrow gali of Mirza Mandi might have looked like a community dominated by conservative patriarchal elders, fostering claustrophobia and monotony in tight physical spaces. In reality there was nothing that was mundane about it.

Life was colourful in its full complexity. Right across from our home lived a family with many unmarried children. The couple whom we called Babaji and Dadi must have had several kids when they were in their mid- to late forties, and these children refused to call their own parents 'Amma' or 'Babu'. They had told their friends that their parents lived elsewhere (or were dead) and were being raised by their *grandparents*. This elderly couple had a daughter in her mid-twenties who left home to live with her friends in a women's hostel. For over a decade she was perpetually enrolled in one degree programme or the other, earning a string of degrees and diplomas. One day, an older child from the neighbourhood whispered, 'Gita aunty is a "homo".' When I asked what it meant, she said, 'When a girl gets married to a girl' or 'when a boy marries another boy'. Growing up in the days of Indira Gandhi's Emergency, with the family planning slogans painted all across the street walls and on the sides of buses, my gut reaction was, 'Great, we certainly need more homos in our country. That would keep our country's population in check.'

And then there was a young boy who lived kitty-corner from us. He lived with his grandmother, an unmarried aunt and his mother whom we called Aunty. Aunty claimed that the eldest son of her next-door neighbour had seduced her with his affections. Knowing that their families would not approve of their inter-caste alliance, they had married in a temple. Her husband had assured her that he would tell his parents about their marriage but had never dared. When she discovered about her pregnancy and told her husband about it, he chickened out. She informed her widowed mother about the incident and proudly assumed the married named of her husband. Not only did she give her son her husband's name, she continued to live in her mother's house across from her *husband's* house for the rest of her life. Whenever she had a quarrel with her mother and sister, she would stand in the balcony shouting slurs at her husband who was not fulfilling his responsibility towards his wife and his son. Her husband who is now in his late seventies has denied this relationship all his life in spite of a striking family resemblance between father and son.

Right around Diwali, when the sky was cluttered with colourful kites, I would see young men – the unmarried bhaiyyas and chachas of the vicinity busy flying kites and shrieking '*yeh kaataa*' or '*voh kaataa*'. They were not only flying kites and cutting the strings of each other's kites through *daanv* and *pench*, but also eyeing, flirting and impressing young unmarried women – sisters and cousins and aunts of their friends and neighbours – severing their parental ties. In the old neighbourhoods, if you were agile and active, you could cross a number of houses from your rooftop. There was no space between the houses, and often the series of vertical niches in the old walls worked like steps that allowed you to jump from one house to another. Many matrimonial alliances and plans to elope and marry were made during Diwali season. Several scandals were brought to my grandmother's attention when lovers from different castes or social classes had made the decision that either they would marry each other or they would die together.

By the time I was a teenager I had learnt that whether it was a love marriage or an arranged marriage, in due time, all couples acted pretty much the same and it was hard to distinguish whether theirs was an arranged or a love marriage. I had also learnt that there was too much pressure on the parents to marry off their daughters. Girls who were constantly 'rejected' lived in constant tension. But so were girls who were 'accepted' by the boy's family. They did not have the freedom to 'reject' a boy if they didn't like him or his family.

My grandmother had the special gift of finding suitable grooms for girls from poor families who had passed their so-called marriageable age or had been rejected because of their ordinary looks. Having married two daughters off in the days of acute financial hardship, my grandmother was sympathetic to those families who were sinking deep in debt to pay for the wedding expenses. In the blasting *loo* of summer months when *Sahalag* (the auspicious season for weddings) was in full swing, she would accompany the parents of a poor bride to local shops to raise funds for the wedding.

Sometimes on Thursday afternoons, I would accompany my grandmother and my aunt to the *mazaar* of Shehzade Miyan. It was located in a small village, several kilometres from our home and it took more than an hour on a cycle rickshaw to get to the nearest road. In order to get to this mazaar, we had to walk through a graveyard, pass by a pond, go through a brick factory, and then walk on a narrow ledge bordering farms covered with bright yellow mustard crop. This shrine was recommended to my grandmother by Amrai Devi when my cousin lost his eyesight and the doctors were unable to restore his vision. My grandmother and my aunt owed their thanks to Shehzade Miyan for making my cousin see again. This mazaar was officiated by a local healer whom everyone called Nawab Sahab and his assistant Gopalji. Bathed in the smell of incense and roses, Nawab Sahab and Gopalji would sit at the foot of Shehzade Miyan's grave, invisible behind the crowd of women who were waiting for their turn to express their woes and receive a cure for their ailment. The taveez they prescribed and the chants they uttered while blowing cool air on the faces of tired, troubled minds had the magical power to ward off all types of physical, psychological and supernatural troubles. Most women came to find solutions to problems connected with either an illness in the family or some issue in their marital life. The latter included, but were not limited to, cheating husbands, daughters being tortured for not being able to bear a child or not being able to give birth to a son, parents-in-law asking for more dowry or sending their daughter-in-law home because of their son having lost interest in his bride.

Occasionally, there were instances of a daughter wanting a separation from her spouse due to sexual incompatibility. The mother would say to Nawab Sahab, 'The boy is very nice. He doesn't drink or gamble and is gainfully employed, but he is *unable to do anything*. Please help so that he can *do something*.'

In a hopeless situation, when Nawab Sahab could not separate the lovers, he would ask the wife to bring an iron knife to the mazaar the following week. He would rotate a bunch of incense on the knife several times, then chant words, blow cool air on her face and then ask the wife to follow him in the nearby woods. They would return after burying the knife. Everyone said that this ritual was for removing the 'other woman' or 'the troublesome in-law' out of the way.

As I grew up I did not behold a rosy picture of marriage. I saw a realistic picture in which women's work – especially those who worked a job, lived in a joint family and took care of their household – was both endless and thankless. Throughout high school and college, when majority of my classmates would carry on about boys and marriage, I was only bored by their talk. Once in a while I would say impatiently, 'Fine, you will get married, then what? You would face the same old drudgery, same old routine that you see in your homes.' There was one girl in my class who loudly proclaimed, 'Marriage is legalized prostitution. We should kill it.' She had no friends.

Sometimes girls would ask among themselves, 'Oh, do you prefer love marriage or arranged marriage?' Most would opt for an arranged marriage, their argument being – 'Parents know the best; they would choose the best.' Or, 'if something went wrong in my marriage, I would always have my parents' support.' I could never understand this 'thank parents for your marriage, blame parents for your marriage' attitude. But the fear of an unsuccessful marriage was immense among those who were focused solely on getting married after completing their studies: 'If I marry against the wishes of my parents, they might have nothing to do with me for life. They would never come to my aid if I needed them.'

A number of girls favoured love marriage, but it had to be within their caste. No one stood up for true love or liked the idea of rebelling against their parents' wishes. Those who voted for love marriage were not sure where they would find their soulmate. How and when that love would occur – would it happen when they left our all-girls school and enrolled in a co-ed university or went to a professional college or at their workplace? The idea of marrying an older brother's friend or a worker at dad's business was definitely an unexciting cliché.

I had also noticed that the love marriages around me that were founded purely on deep physical attraction floundered in a matter of months or years, as that attraction faded. I wondered if it were important to be physically attracted towards someone in order to get married. Or was it intellectual compatibility that formed the basis of a successful marriage? I considered marriage as an important institution, but I didn't think one should marry just in response to social conventions. This notion was in sharp contrast to some of the middle-aged people around me who cautioned, 'Girls who refuse to marry when they are of marriageable age get so frustrated of being single afterwards that they are ready to marry even a rickshawala. Girls should never say no to marriage.'

Thankfully, in my family, there was no pressure to get married. I never overheard any conversations between my parents about how they would marry their daughters or pay for wedding expenses. Their sole focus was providing us with quality education and fostering our creativity. My parents, particularly my father and my grandfather, were always interested in our ideas – projects that we were currently engaged in and were planning to do next.

The question of my marriage never surfaced in my family. When I was eighteen years old, I became seriously ill. For eight months I was in and out of various hospitals. Finally I was diagnosed with a very rare type of autoimmune disease. The word about my illness spread around my community fairly quickly and, as I grew older, my family had assumed that no one would be interested in marrying a sick girl like me. And rightfully so. No proposals came for me. Although, one time, one of our distant relatives said to my mother, 'I would really like Deeksha to be my daughter-in-law but I can't. She is so ambitious and if she were to marry my son, she won't be able to do all the things she wants to do.' My mother remained silent.

In 1995, when I arrived in the United States as a PhD student at Indiana University, I was surprised to see a number of young students already married. Before I came to the US, I had imagined that my fellow classmates might be having boyfriends or live-in relationships, or are dating, but I had not thought that there would be so many American students in their early twenties who would be married.

In due course, I noticed a whole generation of students with divorced parents. Many of my professors were married twice and had children from both marriages. I once asked a senior professor of American studies about this norm and he explained it to me in purely historical terms. He said that the second quarter of the twentieth century was a period of great change in American society. The young men (born between 1915 and 1920) first endured the Great Depression, then faced the wrath of World War II. They saw pain and poverty. In the late 1940s, when the process of rebuilding America started, the generation of young men who had suffered the most wanted to give the best to their children. They were infused with patriotism and strived to create an ideal family portrait. They painted a rosy picture of life before their children, in which there was no discord. By and large, children born in the 1940s grew up with highly romanticized notions about life. They were prepared to do anything for love. A majority of them married young, often without finishing their education; then they had children in quick succession. As their family responsibilities grew, they realized that life was not just about love. They had no professional degrees or careers. Their jobs were low-paying. They needed double incomes to make ends meet. Unlike their mothers, their wives had to work. The everyday struggles connected with job, money and children left them with no energy to enjoy the lives like the way they had imagined. So they quarrelled, sulked and eventually divorced. A decade or more later, when they were more mature and had better understanding of themselves and life around them, they remarried or tried a live-in relationship before they married.

But the children of the subsequent generation (born in the 1960s and 1970s) were not the same. Instead of replicating their parents' actions by marrying young, they wanted to ensure that their marriages truly worked. They stopped rushing into marriage. They dated, tried live-in relationships, and then married the person they loved and were most compatible with.

Even though this interpretation sounds too simplistic, it resonated with what I saw in my American family. In the year 2000, my best friend Eric and I decided to get married. Eric's parents had divorced when he was six and his brother was three years old. When I asked my parents-in-law why they had divorced, they both said the same thing in different ways – they were too young and stupid to get married.

But they were not the only teenagers to get married that young. In the 1960s a large number of young men and women did not even want to wait until they were legally adult, the age of twenty-one, to get married. They wanted to be out of their parents' home (and supervision). Getting married and setting up their own household seemed the easiest way of becoming independent. Young people of that generation wanted to have sex but were afraid to indulge in it since birth control methods then were less reliable. Many young women would get pregnant and then they felt compelled to marry the father of their child. Those who considered themselves as 'sensible' opted to have sex after marriage. So an increasing number of teenagers got married. Many teenagers, like my parents-in-law, eloped to states like Oklahoma, where there was no restriction on minors obtaining a marriage licence. Improved birth control methods have definitely curtailed this impulse of rushing into marriage.

Eric's grandmother, Louise Dyson, was born in 1914 and related very different experiences. She told me that she was twenty years old when she married her husband, Payne Dyson. In her youth, young people did not date; they courted. The couples did not kiss so openly, and if they kissed it was a quick peck on the cheek or on the hand, and very rarely on the lips. Granny Dyson was married for over forty years to her husband. They were very different individuals, who remained in love until Granny's final moments. My mother-in-law says she never saw them argue or quarrel before children, but she had presumed like all married couples they certainly must have had their differences.

Granny believed in marriage. She did not approve of live-in relationships or extramarital sex; but she did not judge people on the basis of those values. Nonetheless, there were some things in her children's generation that 'she just couldn't quite understand', and marriage was certainly one of those things. Even though all of her children had grown up in a very stable family, her two eldest children married in their late teens and divorced within a decade of having their children, and subsequently married and divorced, again and again. Her youngest son did not follow this pattern. He married at the age of twenty-nine, after an extended courtship and engagement that lasted for approximately ten years, and is still married to his wife.

But to say that divorces did not occur in Granny Dyson's generation is also untrue. I once interviewed a weaver by the name of Mary Schmidt in Bloomington, Indiana. She was sixty-seven years old in 1996. Mary had a very lonely childhood in Chicago. She was the only child, and her mother refused to socialize or allow her daughter to play with other children in the neighbourhood. Mary's parents had divorced when she was a year old. In those days, divorce carried a negative stigma, and most people blamed the woman for not being able to 'keep' her husband. Mary's mother never remarried. She kept her daughter away from other children and their families so that no questions would be asked of her father's whereabouts.

In the eighteen years of my marriage, a multitude of cultural stereotypes about American family life that I had harboured had been broken. I feel very fortunate to have spent time with three of my husband's grandparents born between 1910 and 1916. I saw Eric's ageing grandfather Baker actively taking care of his wife, Mildred, when they were both in mid-eighties. Mildred had been diagnosed with multiple sclerosis at the age of forty when her children were still young. She was still a young mother in her early thirties. The issues that granny and granddad Baker faced due to her disability were no different from what my parents dealt with due to my father's muscular dystrophy.

In India, most people still hold the view that there is no depth in American marriage. They believe that American couples have little tolerance towards each other and will file for a divorce for the tiniest of reasons, such as one partner snoring loudly or husband not doing the dishes. They believe these American couples are selfish; they think about themselves and not their children. But now I know this is an over-generalization.

Shortly after I learnt that Eric's parents were divorced, I remarked, 'Oh, I am so sorry. Your poor mother. She was so young. It must be so difficult for her to raise two small children.' Conforming to the cultural stereotype I had about American couples, I had presumed that Eric's father must have left her. He reacted sharply: 'Ms Nagar, what do you know about divorces? You know nothing. So, don't you ever pity my mother like that! I have wonderful parents.' I was shocked by the sharpness of his tone. I bit my tongue and resolved to look at all relationships with a very open mind. I have since never made the mistake of assuming that just because a couple is divorced it means that there is hate and antagonism between them. Of course there are a number of couples that divorce because they have bad quarrels and cannot stand each other. And more couples who do not divorce because of financial dependence, health insurance and other types of bureaucratic issues, and quarrel their entire lives. However, I must say I know more divorced couples who get along better after their divorce. In the twenty-two years I have spent in the United States, I have known numerous parents who are divorced and doing a fabulous job raising their children without fanning spite or hatred towards their former spouses or in-laws. My husband Eric, his younger brothers and our children are deeply attached not only to their parents but also to their grandparents and relatives on either side. Divorce can be hard for children, but experiencing quarrel daily is worse.

In my early twenties, I had fanaticized being married to an idealist – a sensitive man who was engaged in social issues and didn't think about money and material wealth all the time – someone who displayed a great deal of interest in literature and the arts. I didn't try to put a face to my fantasy because I didn't think that such men existed. In terms of my personal ideas of marriage, I considered friendship to be an essential part of marriage. I also wanted marriage to be a beginning and not an end. As a child I always wondered about the story that followed after 'they lived happily ever after'. As an adult, that 'after' became exceedingly important to me. I didn't want to be encased in marriage. My heart rebelled against the idea of a claustrophobic love that suffocates. I associated marriage with love, friendship and freedom. And all of these three associations were equally important to me. I didn't want to be compulsively married to just about anyone because I was going to be thirty.

Eric always cautions me, 'Be careful what you wish for.' I found myself married to a man who had become my best friend, whom I loved and had a strong intellectual connection with. If I had not met Eric, in all probability I wouldn't have married and taken on the daunting task of going back and forth between the United States and India. Marriage as an institution, and what we have made of it, troubles me deeply. The oppression, violence, suffocation, dependence, and physical and emotional trauma guised in marriage is unnerving. Perhaps marriage is not for everyone. We need to eliminate the physio-psychological pressure involved in getting married. I, as someone who had never imagined myself to be married, am married to a man who was a confirmed bachelor. To me, our togetherness feels like a journey. A journey in which we can map our own path and make necessary stops at our own pace. A journey through life, where there is no competition to excel and no pressure of being judged by others. We have to warn our child that we are an atypical family. We have lived apart, before and after marriage, for many years because of my studies and jobs in different states; we have lived through bouts of my prolonged illness that seem to last forever, and months of separation during the time I spent in India for personal and professional matters. When I am ill, Eric becomes my primary caregiver; when I am in India, he becomes the single parent taking care of the minutest details of our family's needs in a servant-less society. There is nothing easy about the life that we have chosen to live. But we live through all of these challenges with good humour. For our child, this is the normal life – observing, discovering and discussing intercultural differences are a part of our everyday routine.

I accept our differences in our togetherness. I am awestruck by the complexity of human nature – how we mature and are constantly growing in terms of ideas, attitudes and philosophies about life. There is so much mystery in life and the world of relationship that we weave for ourselves. I do not think marriage is just about knowing or understanding each other, it is about discovering and rediscovering ourselves, our friendships, and the relationships that make us who we are in every phase of life. If anyone were to ask me what constitutes a successful marriage, I would have to say that it is the ever-growing friendship and humour. Trust, love, faith, respect and all the other things that we value follow from that source.

The Cost of a Runaway Marriage

NEHA DIXIT

In January 2014, Samit, a thirty-year-old film editor in Delhi got a phone call. His girlfriend Mohini was twenty-four and worked as a subeditor of an Assamese newspaper in Guwahati. The phone call was from her father who'd just found out about their secret long-distance relationship. 'He told me that if I didn't call off the relationship, he'd inform his ULFA contacts and get rid of both me and Mohini,' Samit says.

Funny? Empty threats? Not so much. Back in Guwahati, Mohini was forced to quit her job. She was locked at home for a week until she finally ran away from home and jumped on a train to Delhi. In Delhi, 2,000 kilometres away, they weren't safe. Samit recalls: 'Mohini's cousins in Delhi traced us. We urgently needed to get married but we had no money to.'

On 16 May 2014, the day India elected its new government, Pradeepa, a twenty-three-year-old engineering student in

Namakkal district, Tamil Nadu, was denied examination hall tickets because she had converted to Islam to marry a man of her choice. A second-year civil engineering student, she had fallen in love with J. Fazil, a twenty-three-year-old fellow student. On 12 April [2014], she'd married him under sharia law and their marriage certificate was issued by a government-appointed qazi the same day. Of all the problems they anticipated, not being able to take their exams was not one of them.

Manish, twenty-three, fell in love with Khurshida, nineteen, in Nilokheri village of Karnal, Haryana. In this Jat-dominated village, there were five Dalit Muslim families who lived on the outskirts of the village. They were treated as untouchables. When Manish and Khurshida finally eloped to get married in January 2014, Manish's landowning feudal father approached the khap panchayat in the village, which in turn alerted the Muslim khap panchayat in the vicinity. 'We went to the mosque because I wanted to convert to Islam for the sake of getting married. They held Khurshida hostage and called the members of both the khap panchayats. Somehow, we escaped before they arrived,' he recalls. The news had spread across villages in the next few hours. 'No temple was ready to convert Khurshida to Hinduism to get us married. It had almost become a communal issue in the area,' he says.

A couple of years ago, when I was protesting against my extended family's attempts to find me a match, one of my aunts said, 'If you want to go for love marriage, we have no problem. It will only save us money.' To my youthful sensibilities, it seemed the most obnoxious response ever. This year I remembered what my aunt said. Here's why.

Around the time Samit and Mohini were in trouble, my partner N and I had decided to get married, much to our friends' disappointment. They thought we'd failed them by succumbing to the patriarchal institution of marriage to guard our companionship. But we'd weighed it up and thought it was practical to get married – to be able to manage our crumbling finances better, to be able to live with each other without lying to landlords and real-estate agents, to check in to the same room in small-town hotels without scandalizing staff. We'd decided to pick our battles.

Since both of us are non-believers, we decided we'd get married under the Special Marriage Act (SMA), 1954. The SMA was enacted by Parliament to provide a special kind of marriage for all Indian nationals in India and in foreign countries, irrespective of the religion or faith followed by either party. It provides equal inheritance and divorce rights to both women and men.

My extended family was, surprisingly, easily convinced. They didn't particularly care for my loud opposition to patriarchal rituals. In fact, they had an excellent patriarchal reason to accept it. They thought civil marriage was most suitable for me, with my father being dead. Who'd make the painful and expensive arrangements for a 'normal' wedding? One of the only few dear aunts I have even told me, secretly, 'Perfect decision. Otherwise you'd have to do your pheras and supervise the ghee for the hawan also.'

We were lucky not to be rushed into marriage.

In Chennai, the very young Pradeepa and Fazil wanted to get married right away because they were facing plenty of opposition from both parents. Pradeepa's parents were threatening her to get her married off to a boy of their choice. 'We'd heard that the court procedures are longer so we decided to go for the Islamic method which took less than half a day,' she explains. She says, 'I had no choice but to convert. That was the only way to get married quickly.'

It was a month later that her college, Pavai College of Technology, told her that she and her new husband would not get hall tickets as they objected to her conversion to Islam and her inter-religious wedding. It was only after the Madras High Court intervened a week later that the college issued the couple hall tickets.

In India, more and more young people are exerting their choice when it comes to whom they marry. Breaking caste, language and religious barriers – they often court the displeasure and sometimes vengeance of their families. Sometimes just the decision to exert their choice invites punishment that ranges from emotional blackmail, ostracizing over years, all the way to murder. Across the country, particularly in north Indian states like Haryana, Rajasthan and Uttar Pradesh, numerous couples who have decided to marry on their own have been killed either on the diktats of khap panchayats or of their own families.

In the past, Hindu right-wing outfits like the Bajrang Dal and the Sri Ram Sene have not just taken pride in threatening couples who break caste or religious barriers, but have also increased their visibility by doing so. They've formed groups like the Hindu Kanya Raksha Samiti and issued death threats to inter-caste couples.

They have accused Muslim men of carrying out a malicious campaign of conversion through seduction and marriage – aka Love Jihad.

Just a week after Pradeepa's exam hall surprise and two days before Prime Minister Narendra Modi's swearing-in ceremony, the Vishwa Hindu Parishad (VHP), an affiliate organization of the winning BJP, presented a legal prohibition on 'horizontal religious conversions' as one of the top priorities on its wish list to the new government. ('Horizontal' conversion in the VHP lexicon refers to changing from one faith to another.)

This brazen cocktail of ruthless fathers, busybody cousins and violent religious organizations does have one happy by-product: the lucrative business of organizing weddings for runaway couples. A business that I was to get to know intimately rather soon.

How to be civil in marriage. Or not.

Our first visit to make an inquiry about the proceedings should have warned us. The entrance to the newly constructed Saket court complex in south Delhi, next to mammoth shopping malls, is fenced with lawyers in black coats, clutching thin stacks of files. Each time a new entrant passes through the security gate, they break into a song of '*Challan-bail-shaadi-affidavit-haan ji-Challan-bail-shaadi-affidavit-haan ji?*'

As we pushed through the passage towards the enquiry section to find out the procedure for a civil marriage, a thin, short man with neatly oiled hair moved towards us. His eyes had judged us and found us wanting. 'Sir, at least say what you want. You want to get married?'

'Yes,' I said.

'Do you want to know the procedure? Come with me, no charges for explaining,' he said.

We looked at each other in approval and agreed to be explained to.

Om Prakash, in his early thirties, from Bareilly, Uttar Pradesh, was pleased to learn that I was from UP too. Three of us walked towards the lawyers' chambers. The paan stains on the newly constructed yellow spiral staircase were so uniform that they seemed like art. Giant photos of candidates for the Bar

Council elections wished a happy Dussehra, Diwali, Eid, Guru Parv, Christmas, New Year and Republic Day to the visitors – all in one go. There couldn't have been a more assuring token display of secularism – as it turned out, the last token display of secularism that day.

Om Prakash took us to a narrow chamber on the third floor shared by three more lawyers. He placed himself on a chair behind the farthest table and asked us to join him.

'Now tell me your exact requirement,' he said, thumping the table.

'We are here for a civil marriage,' N said.

'No problem. It can be done,' he said in a reassuring tone.

'How long does the whole procedure take?' N asked.

'One week.'

'Just one week? What are the requirements?' N asked. We had heard that the Special Marriage Act takes a month.

'Two garlands, two witnesses, your date-of-birth certificate and residence proof.'

'Garlands for what?' N was a bit foxed.

'We will take you to the Arya Samaj mandir, get the two of you to exchange garlands and do a hawan. Once the pujari issues the marriage certificate and we get the pictures, we will submit the application in the court. The judge will call you in the next ten days for approval,' he explained.

'No, but we want a court wedding not an Arya Samaj wedding,' I said.

'This *is* a court wedding,' he argued.

'Under Special Marriage Act,' I said emphatically.

'Wait, what is your name?' he asked pointing his finger towards me.

'Neha Dixit.'

'And what is yours?' he asked N.

'N Sawhney.'

'Hmm. That's what. Sawhney and Dixit. Both will come under Hindu Marriage Act. This is safe, don't worry. Parents will not even come to know,' he said.

'No, our parents will be a part of it. We want a civil marriage.'

'Why? Both of you are Hindus.'

'I am not a Hindu. Technically, I am a Sikh,' N corrected him.

'But Sikh is also Hindu!' He clapped his hands in triumph. N told me after that, for a moment, that he was distracted by an irrational rage at Om Prakash's cavalier dismissal of the entire Khalistan movement. Recently, the Anand Marriage Act, 2014, was announced for registration of Sikh couples. Until then, Sikh couples abroad who didn't want to be identified as Hindu were stymied by marriage certificates issued under the Hindu Marriage Act.

'No, we don't want a religious wedding,' N said.

'Why? Both of you are Hindus. Why should Hindus run from Hinduism, Nehaji? You are from my part of the world. You'll wear *ver-meee-llion* after the wedding anyway. So what's the big deal?' He gave me a slimy grin.

'No, I will not,' I replied.

This was clearly a blow to his conception of what a decent girl from his part of the world is like. But he continued the conversation. 'But it's not possible. Two Hindus can only marry under the Hindu Marriage Act.'

'Why not the Special Marriage Act?' N asked.

'That's for different religions. You cannot go for it unless one of you converts to some other religion like Islam or Christianity,' said Om Prakash.

'But we don't believe in any religion at all. We are atheists, agnostics – something like that,' said N.

Om Prakash had an expression – like the hapless hero of a Ramsay horror who'd discovered that the sultry heroine was actually a witch. 'That's very difficult. There is no provision to convert to atheism.'

We looked at each other. I could see N was *done*. I could also see he was irritated with me for looking like I was willing to negotiate, for not storming out.

'What is the procedure to get married under the Hindu Marriage Act?' I asked.

'As I explained earlier, we can get it done quickly. We charge twenty-five thousand rupees, which includes Arya Samaj–mandir expenses, affidavits, attestation by a gazetted officer, a photographer to take your pictures and a wedding card as a proof of your wedding. Next day, we will file for registration.'

We left.

Om Prakash and his associate Bhagwan Jha claim to conduct 15–20 such weddings every month. Most of his clients are 'runaway couples' who are often in a hurry to get married for fear of non-consenting parents, as in the case of Samit and Mohini, sometimes even seeking protection from the court because their families have threatened to kill them. These couples on the run often don't enjoy the luxury of rejecting Om Prakash, of finding a way to celebrate their marriage in a way that affirms their own belief systems. They are told that the usual process entails an Arya Samaj wedding, and that's what they get.

Then there's the cost. Based on our spot poll of all the touts at the Saket court and through online consultations, we put together a current rate list for 'runaway' couples to get married:

Arya Samaj wedding

Basic wedding: Rs 5,000–8,000

Wedding, materials and photographer: Rs 10,000

Combo package, including a wedding and court registration: Rs 15,000–20,000

Combo package with two witnesses and complete documents: Rs 22,000–25,000

Combo package with two witnesses and complete documents, all in one day: Rs 40,000–50,000

Combo package, two witnesses, complete documents and police protection, all in one day: Rs 65,000–75,000

Muslim wedding

Since government registration is still not mandatory for Muslim couples, the legal services double up as matrimony facilitators for mixed couples where one of the partners wishes to convert to Islam. Muslim weddings are conducted and approved by qazis.

Marriage with certificate: ≥Rs 10,000

Marriage with certificate and conversion of one partner to Islam: Rs 30,000

Marriage with certificate, conversion and police protection: Rs 35,000–70,000, depending on the availability of documents

Marriages between Muslims, Hindus and Christians under the Special Marriage Act (SMA)

Application submission with attestations and affidavits: Rs 6,000–10,000

Application with attestations, affidavits and supporting identity documents: Rs 25,000

All-in-one, including three witnesses and complete documents: Rs 25,000–Rs 35,000

All-in-one with police protection: Rs 40,000–Rs 70,000

When Mohini caught the getaway train to Delhi, Samit didn't have a stable job at the time, nor proof of residence in Delhi. They couldn't afford the going rates to get married. 'We sought help from Love Commandos [a group that offers help to eloping couples] who were ready to rob us of whatever we had,' he says. Samit says the Love Commandos asked for Rs 10,000. When some friends stepped in with money they could finally get married – in an Arya Samaj mandir.

Going to the Arya Samaj. Gonna get married

Before the Hindu Marriage Act was passed in 1955, which allowed inter-caste marriages and equal divorce rights to men and women, people who wanted to remain Hindus but marry across caste could only do so under the Arya Marriage Validation Act of 1937. Arya Samaj marriages were used more as a euphemism for 'irregular marriages'. Apart from inter-caste marriages, the Arya Marriage Validation Act allowed the marriages of widows and converts from other religions, after a *shuddhi*.

In case of a Hindu and a non-Hindu marrying, the conversion to Hinduism is done after a controversial 'purification' ritual called *shuddhi* executed by the Arya Samaj temple priests. Thereafter, the couple goes to the district court for registration under the Hindu Marriage Act along with age proof, residential proof and two witnesses. After that, couples who fear violence from their families can apply to the high court for police protection.

Not that protection from the law is guaranteed even to couples who enter holy matrimony. In January this year [2014], the Punjab and Haryana High Court passed an unusual judgment. Justice Paramjeet Singh, on hearing the plea of a runaway couple seeking court protection, asked the groom to make a fixed deposit of Rs 2 lakhs in the bride's name and present the receipt in the court. The court's intention, according to a news report, was to '[gauge] the bona fides of the grooms and the genuineness of the relationship after judging the monetary competence of the groom to carry on with the relationship and their willingness to deposit the money in the bride's name.' Justice Singh added that the court had come across cases where girls returned to their parents after being robbed of their 'chastity'. 'Can procurers and panders be allowed to lure innocent young girls in full bloom and put their lives in peril? This is the question this court is confronted with. Another question is how to combat the hideous monster, the masked man, to protect the safety and purity of womanhood.' The couple got married in a temple but their plea for court protection was turned down.

As if this wasn't enough, the courts have gone one step further in characterizing marriages where two adults have made their own choice. In 2011, a bench comprising justices Dalip Singh and Sajjan Singh Kothari of the Rajasthan High Court stated that marriages based on the right to choose, more generally known as love marriages, were examples of 'lust and greed'! The judges remarked, 'The pious purpose of the Arya Samaj mission has been lost sight at by local units in the state and they are becoming a tool for pacification of "greed and lust" for girl and boy, and once it is over the marriage lands in courts resulting in irreversible breakdowns.' And that: 'It takes them one hour to solemnise a marriage between an 18-year-old girl and a 38- or 40-year-old gentleman, which leaves scars forever in the life of parents who bring up their children with great passion and aspirations. Such marriages in lust and greed by young blood cannot be said to be correct.'

It is in the same spirit that on 9 May 2013, a bench of the Uttarakhand High Court delivered a judgment barring the Arya Samaj from issuing marriage certificates to couples. This makes the state, which is accountable for upholding the constitutional rights of citizens, complicit in regressive, patriarchal extra-constitutional practices.

Pandit Vidyadhar Shastri, who is the chief priest at the Arya Samaj mandir in Saket, Delhi, says, 'We do solemnize weddings of a number of eloped couples. In our personal capacity we may have problems with them hurting the feelings of their parents, but in principle we do not turn down any such request. In fact, we have engaged lawyers ourselves to facilitate it for the couples.'

In Nilokheri village, young Manish and Khurshida didn't know what to do. Conversion was not working out. And they didn't know any other way to get married.

A friend told them to get in touch with the All India Democratic Women's Association (AIDWA), the women's wing of the Communist Party of India (Marxist) who have helped such couples in the past. 'We didn't have money to run away to another city nor were we educated enough to know the government procedures. Both the communities were chasing us and saying that what we were doing was illegal. We couldn't believe it was so difficult to be with each other,' says Khurshida.

Jagmati Sangwan, the national vice president of AIDWA, who has tirelessly fought for twenty years against the atrocities of khap panchayats in Haryana and ensured human rights for over 200 such couples, is of the view that the state has very often failed its citizens by not just pushing them towards religious patriarchal structures in matters of love but has also indulged in moral policing itself. AIDWA activists worked hard to pacify the family members and the khaps to ensure that neither community looked at it as a case of religious conversion in the 'garb of love marriage'.

Sangwan says, 'We got Manish and Khurshida married under the Special Marriage Act tactically, to prevent what was taking the shape of a communal issue. The families have dissociated themselves with the couple, but at least so many lives were saved from a communal riot in the area.' In January 2014, after getting married, Khurshida and Manish moved to Delhi.

Sangwan says, 'Courts, khap panchayats and right-wing groups have been similar [in their treatment of] the couples. All demand parents' validation for consenting adults to choose their life partners. It's because of the lack of state support [that] couples are forced to run away to other cities, making themselves all the more vulnerable to scamsters who take them to Arya Samaj temples and mosques and con them without legal proof of marriage. Communal issues are also unnecessarily often flared up in cases of inter-religious marriages for lack of state support.'

It is in this context that the Special Marriage Act (SMA), 1954, is not just an important tool for consenting adults but also integral to the larger secular structure of India.

A very special marriage act

The Special Marriage Act (SMA) embodies all contradictions of liberal citizenship. It is a civil and secular law of marriage. It has been argued that the SMA will be a basis for the future Uniform Civil Code (UCC) in India, which has been recently brought back to the fore by the newly elected NDA government.

Scholars also claim that SMA, in the current form, is seen as being more aligned with feminist principles of marriage, inheritance and divorce as compared to the UCC, which caters to patriarchal Hindu family values. Naveen T.K., a legal academic who teaches at IIT Delhi, says, 'SMA can definitely provide a framework or a template for UCC, but the triumph of SMA remains in the fact that it is not dominated by the Hindu majority laws or the right wing.'

Perveez Mody in her excellent book *The Intimate State: Love Marriage and the Law in Delhi*, which documents the role of the laws of the land in cases of self-choice marriages in Delhi, writes, 'It is noteworthy that SMA and uniform civil code were both opposed together in the Parliament in 1951 because they were seen as a threat to "Hindu India".'

In the Supreme Court's abstract discussion of the value of 'inter-caste, inter-religion, and inter-region marriages' for 'promoting national unity', its decision cited that the Special Marriage Act of 1954 can be used for such marriages, as well as the Hindu Marriage Act of 1955, which, by adopting a quite broad definition of 'Hindu', can be used for marriages between Hindus, Buddhists, Jains and Sikhs.

The SMA is also seen as woman-friendly in the sense that it limits the application of personal law in family affairs. In India, family affairs like marriage, divorce and succession are governed by a different set of laws according to faith which are known as personal laws. Divorce by triple talaq does not apply to Muslim women married under SMA. Women across religions are entitled to equal inheritance compared to personal laws. According to legal experts, the Indian Succession Act is applicable to both men and women married under the Special Marriage Act, which is far more egalitarian than the personal laws.

The SMA was originally Act III of 1872. It was introduced by Henry Sumner Maine, a British comparative jurist and historian. Maine is well-known for his thesis that in ancient societies individuals were tied to the status of traditional groups. In the modern one, the thesis argues, individuals are seen as autonomous agents who are free to make contracts or associations with whomever they choose.

Meshing with this worldview, Henry Maine's Act III of 1872 permitted 'any dissenters [from religion] to marry whomever they chose under the new civil marriage law'. The puritanical administrators and representatives from the local government in India responded with disdain and opposed Maine's bill. They were of the view that the particular legislation would not just lead to immorality but also encourage marriages based on lust.

Religion and Personal Law in Secular India, a 2001 book edited by Gerald James Larson, mentions that independent India introduced an element of choice while retaining personal laws through the SMA, 1954: 'The Special Marriage Act of 1872 had provided a code of general law under which couples could choose to marry and divorce, but in order to utilize this option they had to affirm that neither was a Christian, Jew, Hindu or Muslim. In effect they had to renounce their religious and property relations with their families. In 1954, Parliament passed a new Special Marriage Act that eliminated the onerous renunciatory costs of availing of civil marriage.'

The SMA, 1954, allowed individuals the freedom to defy both caste and religion in the case of marriage. While the bill was being argued, the SMA was seen as being for the westernized urban elite, while the Hindu Marriage Act, was seen as being for the larger majority. At the time, several MPs objected that the law was destroying society by facilitating inter-caste marriages and hurting the idea of family by introducing divorce.

In contemporary times, the process of a civil marriage in India, however, is subject to a number of conditions – conditions that negate the Supreme Court's 2006 judgment's dream of abolishing the caste and religious divide through inter-caste marriage.

According to the law, any pair of unmarried, sane, consenting adults, where the bridegroom is over twenty-one years of age and the bride is over eighteen, and who are unrelated within the degrees of prohibited relationship irrespective of faith or caste, can get married under the SMA. The only exception is in the state of Jammu and Kashmir, where it does not apply. It shouldn't cost anything and requires no ritual.

However, the SMA has its own shortcomings. Touts like Om Prakash and Bhagwan Jha were a clear window into the conditions under which many couples who want a court wedding never get a chance to negotiate their right to get married under the secular SMA. In my case, where we had the luxury of time and money, and the opportunity to figure out what we really believed in, it was still not very easy to get endorsed by this law. After we ditched the touts and their many wares there was still a lot to trudge through in pursuit of our secular dream.

As a nation drunk on Bollywood weddings, it is only runaway couples who we see get married in court in films, be it the famous *Bombay* or the flop *Ahista Ahista*, where the protagonist earns his living by appearing as a witness to the marriages of eloped couples in court. Popular culture has therefore conveniently marginalized the SMA instead of bringing it into mainstream culture.

We had to furnish copies of our passports to establish permanent addresses, our PAN card copies, our class 10 certificates to prove our age, and copies of our rent agreement, electricity and water bill. Also, while the Supreme Court noted in September 2013 that the Aadhaar card was not mandatory for marriage registration, apart from other things, the notification of the judgment had not reached the lower courts in January 2014. This is why we were also required to give copies of our Aadhar cards, for which we had to run one more marathon to acquire. Additionally, since one of us had given a rent agreement copy, we needed a separate round of police verification and a guarantee from the neighbours that they had known me for over six months. We were also required to furnish the identity proof, Aadhar card copies and photos of three witnesses (as compared to two under the Hindu Marriage Act) a full month in advance.

In Delhi, 55 per cent of citizens still do not have a ration card, the most basic identity card. In comparison, the need for the above listed documents is a clear attempt at marginalizing SMA to a privileged small group.

But troubles don't end with acquiring these documents. As soon as the complete application is submitted in court, one set of notices announcing your intention to marry is pasted outside the marriage office. And another set is dispatched – hold your breath – to the families of the two parties. This is done thirty days in advance to invite objections, if any, from acquaintances and family. Interestingly, unlike the SMA, no such notice is required in 'regular' religious marriages. All states in India except Delhi follow this infantilizing practice.

In a landmark judgment by Justice S. Ravindra Bhat of the Delhi High Court in April 2009, the practice of sending notices to the homes of couples desirous of solemnizing their marriage under the SMA was curbed. But in practice, it still continues in most Delhi courts as officials fear the wrath of the parents of the couples or moral policing groups.

An official in the magistrate's office, who did not wish to be identified, said to me, 'There are anti–love jihad groups who are regulars here checking for inter-religious weddings. They then inform the parents of the couple.'

Another report suggests that the administrations in Ghaziabad, Noida and Gurgaon, in the states of Uttar Pradesh and Haryana, insist on illegally dispatching these notices but are not willing to bear the expenses of doing so. They insist that couples provide pre-addressed, pre-stamped envelopes beforehand. Couples in these towns have to publish an advertisement of their proposed marriage in a leading newspaper and submit a copy of the published advertisement to the office of the marriage officer.

In Gurgaon, the deputy commissioner's office has taken pains to add a column for specifying the applicants' religion in the 'intent to marry' form and an additional point about the citizenship of the applicants in the declaration form.

Sangwan has recently appealed to the Haryana government, asking that the thirty-day-rule under SMA be done away with. She says, 'SMA in its present form is no different from the khap panchayats. Both ask for parents' consent. Moreover, its complicated proceedings force the majority of couples on the run, confronted by various hostile and complex socio-political pressures, to opt for a religious form of marriage.'

The number of SMA marriages is fairly low when compared to religious ones. A 2002 media report suggested that in a period of one year, while 1,100 marriages were registered under Hindu Marriage Act in Chandigarh, only forty-nine marriages were registered under the SMA in a period of ten months.

Another fallout of the complicated procedures and general atmosphere of transgression is the rising number of illegal inter-religious marriages, especially in Tamil Nadu. In the hurry to get married, many couples who registered under the Tamil Nadu Registration of Marriages Act (TNRMA), 2009, and managed to get married the same day realized years later that their marriage was invalid.

After spending close to Rs 5,000 in running costs, on the day we submitted our application to the Mehrauli Badarpur Magistrate's office, the additional district magistrate asked, 'Why do you want to marry under the SMA when you can marry under the Hindu Marriage Act? Such a complicated procedure!'

I was about to explain the logic when N, anticipating further trouble, cut me short and manufactured the reason, 'Sir, my parents want us to marry under the Sikh customs and her parents want us to marry under the Hindu customs. That is why we have convinced them of our marriage under the SMA.'

'Oh, okay. That makes sense,' he replied.

Religion triumphed over rationality and our application was accepted.

(This essay is used with permission from Yahoo originals, *where it first appeared, on 23 July 2014.)*

Mixed Media Marriage

Bulbul Sharma

The Banerjees were on high alert. Their youngest daughter, Neela, had just announced her intention to marry a non-Bengali boy.

'I knew this would happen when you allowed her to cut her hair,' said Dida from her corner.

'Ma, that was fifteen years ago – when she was ten years old.'

'That is how the rot sets in early,' she said snapping her betal nut–cutter angrily. 'Non-Bengali blood will now flow freely in our family. Who knows who your other daughter will marry … maybe a Chinese man?' the old lady said enjoying the shocked look on her daughter-in-law's face.

Neela, the bride to be, stood firm as a rock. In fact, later when the dust had settled down, her family nickname became 'Rock', and all the younger members of the Banerjee clan quoted her whenever a family dispute over a mixed marriage arose.

'Remember Rock?' they would say to settle matters amicably.

On this gentle spring morning, Neela's parents were shocked by her sudden decision to get married to a man whose family was not known to them at all. She had not picked a nice, well-behaved Punjabi boy whose family had lived in Kolkata and spoke fluent Bengali. No. She had gone all out and chosen a true Punjabi from Punjab.

It was frightening. Their daughter was recklessly embarking on a journey into an unknown, unfamiliar, unchartered zone. Marrying outside the community was a dangerous thing. Who was this boy? Who were his parents?

'Is he educated?' asked an uncle who had just finished writing a three-volume tome on the history of the Brahmins – in Bengal – where else.

'Punjabi ... means he wears a turban?' asked a nephew nervously. He had once got into a fight with a Sikh boy in school and fared very badly.

'I had a friend in school who married a Punjabi. He pushed her off the terrace one day when she refused to cook some black dal for him. Luckily they lived on the second floor and she only broke a leg,' said a neighbour who had dropped in as soon as she had heard the bad news.

'All you people are really living in the Middle Ages. People marry outside their community all the time now,' said Neela's younger sister, who was in love with a Malayali boy and was grateful to her sister for clearing her path. Today Punjabi, tomorrow Malayali.

'This will be the first time in our family, you know,' said Neela's mother quietly. A great-uncle had married a German lady in 1930 but that wonderful woman spoke, thought and cooked like a true Bengali. She always wore a sari and everyone forgot that she was not one of them till she died and was buried instead of being cremated. 'She was so nice and well-behaved, we never imagined she was not Bengali,' the Banerjee clan said.

Neela's mother was anxious about what the older members of the clan would say. Her husband had already called a Banerjee emergency meeting and all the relatives were coming for lunch the next day. A serious matter like this could only be resolved over food.

In a sunny verandah filled with drying cauliflower garlands, Vikram, the bridegroom-to-be faced his mother's wrath.

'Hai Bhagwan ... Bengali ... what for...? What about all the lovely, fair Punjabi girls here in Ludhiana?' she cried, beating her ample bosom.

'I knew this would happen the day you bought him all those fat books,' hissed his grandmother from her charpoy. 'Always reading ... instead of playing and fighting with other boys like a proper man.'

'Is she dark?' asked his aunt.

'Does she look like Bipasha Basu?' asked his younger brother.

'You want your children to grow up eating fish curry? Eating rice with their fingers? Over my dead body,' said his grandmother wondering whether she should throw a fit now or wait for a more appropriate moment when there was a larger audience.

'Son, it is your choice but think carefully. These mixed marriages do not last, you know. My good friend married a south Indian ... from Madras I think, and she cooked only in coconut oil, put coconut oil in her hair and on her body. He had a nervous breakdown eventually ... saw coconuts everywhere. Healthy, hatta-katta fellow reduced to a skeleton within months,' said Vikram's father.

'She is Bengali, Papaji,' said Vikram.

'Same thing ... Bengali ... Madrasi ... All different from us, beta. Punjabis are the best people in India.'

'Remember … what Bengal thinks today … India thinks tomorrow,' said the uncle to Neela every morning hoping these wise words etched on every true son of Bengal's heart would convince her to change her mind.

Neela and Vikram ignored all the parental onslaught which now flew at them from all directions. 'A really bad idea … will not work … break up the family … what will everyone say?' And then flowed the emotional blackmailing.

'I will die; you will be sorry then … it will break Dadi/Nani/Didima/Dadu/Thakuma's heart.'

'How can you do this to us?'

'You will see my dead face' (*'Tumi amar mora mukh dekhbe'*).

And then as the news spread came more angry extended family outbursts.

From the Kapoors:

'Fish, fish, fish – all the time now for you, beta.'

'How will you tolerate the smell of mustard oil in your kitchen?'

'Your children will be so dark.'

'You will have to listen to that wailing, sad music all day.'

'Bengali women are very bossy. She will really dominate you.'

From the Banerjee side:

'You will eat rajma chawal all your life now.'

'You will forget Robindra Sangeet.'

'You will forget how to read, write, speak Bengali.'

'Your children will be wild, uncultured and will never learn to sing, dance or paint.'

'Your husband will throw you off from the rooftop.'

'Punjabi men are so aggressive. He will dominate you.'

Finally the wedding date was fixed. And after much discussion and debate the venue for the wedding was agreed upon as Delhi, since it was declared a neutral territory. The Banerjees arrived, all twenty-six of the immediate family, by train on a cold February morning while the Kapoors travelled by bus. All thirty-five of them by Volvo bus from Chandigarh.

Both parties clashed at the venue – a small guest house hired by Vikram and Neela. The battle began in the wedding hall.

Each side had brought its own priest who now faced each other like boxing opponents.

The Punjabi priest chanted with his eyes wide open talking all the time on his mobile phone, while the aged Bengali priest who had conducted countless Banerjee weddings, funerals and mukhe bhath (first food) ceremonies kept his eyes shut in disapproval.

The families sat opposite each other muttering under their breath. The Bengali women had come dressed in rustling silk saris, and the men had worn their best silk dhotis and kurtas which had finely hand-wrinkled sleeves – a must-have for all aristocratic Bengali men.

'They should have had their clothes ironed at least,' said a Kapoor aunt.

'Why are they all wearing monkey caps? It is not that cold. Look, even their "pandit" has covered his head and nose with one funny cap,' remarked another member of the clan.

'So much gold jewellery. Must be artificial,' she proclaimed with knowing finality.

The Punjabis had come dressed in their shining best, and the men outshone the women as they strutted about in their beautiful gleaming 'sherwanis' and gold-embroidered stoles.

'Why are the men dressed like women?' asked a Bengali uncle pulling his cap over his forehead.

The chanting began in a cacophony of confusion as the priests clashed once more. Each tried to out-chant the other and the couple somehow managed to understand the conflicting instructions: 'Throw flower' ... 'No ... Do not throw'; 'place your right hand' ... 'place your left hand'; 'keep her face covered with the betel leaves' ... 'No! cover her head with her sari'; 'exchange garlands now' ... 'No, stop ... lift the bride on the platform first'.

They were finally married after two exhausting hours each side convinced that their priest had won.

Suddenly the Bengalis, many of whom had fallen asleep during the lengthy ceremony, were jolted off their seats. A tall, lanky DJ now appeared in a glittering gold suit and 'bangra-rock' filled the wedding hall. The Bengalis looked shell-shocked as the loud music rattled the glass windows, except for an old uncle who was quite deaf and slept on.

They watched with horror as one by one the Kapoors jumped up to dance. Plump aunts twirled with abandon; children leapt with joy and even the grandmother twisted and turned gracefully in their midst.

'Come on ... yaar, join us...' said one Kapoor to a Banerjee. They refused, embarrassed by this public display of bad dancing to terrible music.

'Dance is a sacred art form. This is like a monkey circus,' said the erudite Banerjee uncle turning his face away.

'It looks fun though,' said the nephew who liked the look of one very pretty Punjabi girl who was the best dancer he had ever seen.

Suddenly he rose and crossed over to the enemy side and began dancing with hesitant steps. His family gave a huge collective sigh.

'See how they corrupt our young with their uncultured ways,' said the uncle.

The renegade nephew was greeted with shouts of glee, thumped on his back, and soon he was the centre of the Punjabi dancers. Neela, pleased that someone had made an effort, watched her new family happily. They certainly knew how to have fun. She wished her father and uncles did not look so uncomfortable sitting in a row with gloomy faces like people in a dentist's waiting room. Vikram had tried so hard to talk to them but they all seem to be in mourning.

Then dinner was announced. The Bengalis wearing unhappy faces like a losing cricket team ambled to the table.

'There will be Punjabi food, what else? That black "maa'dal" which they like so much. We should have never agreed to hold the wedding outside Kolkata.' Mumbled Neela's mother unhappily.

'Yes, at home we could have had five kinds of fish, kosha mangsho ... papaya chutney ... homemade sandesh...' said the aunt dragging her feet to the table.

The Punjabis gathered around the table in silence. They had expected fish, fish and fish. One aunt had even had her dinner at home.

'They will have that foul-smelling mustard fish which will give me indigestion.'

The table was laden from one end to the other with Chinese food. There were plates piled with Hakka noodles, Singapore chicken glistening with red capsicums, huge prawns in garlic sauce, and many other dishes with heady, fragrant flavours which were neither Punjabi nor Bengali.

At first the wedding parties on both sides did not know what to say and then one young Bengali nephew and his pretty new-found Punjabi friend gave a shout of approval 'yummy Chinese' and began to attack the food.

One by one the rest of the clan began eating. They knew this was neutral food which neither party could find fault with. As they ate they talked to each other and soon they were laughing and exchanging views. Their fear and suspicion of each other was still there, but they could see a faint glimmer of something good and kind on the other side.

'These Punjabi women really know how to dance,' said the erudite uncle. 'It is like a folk art form for them.'

'I like the way the Bengali men talk. So serious and they seem to know everything,' said an aunt.

Neela and Vikram sat together in one corner of the wedding hall. 'They look all right now ... the Hakka noodles seem to have worked. That was a good idea I had,' said Vikram.

'It was my idea,' said Neela.

'Not really.' Vikram smiled.

'Anyway ... This is only for now. They will start complaining once more very soon,' muttered Neela.

'The trouble with you Bengalis is that you argue about everything,' said Vikram.

'What about you Punjabis? So loud and aggressive. Bangra, bangra all the way,' said Neela.

'We know how to enjoy life; we also know how to work hard,' Vikram retorted.

'We use our brains. We value education and not just money. We are sensitive people,' Neela said.

'Too sensitive, too proud and too lazy to do honest day's work. Look at all the beggars in Kolkata.'

'We treat our women much better...' said Neela, raising her voice.

Their families watched them and shook their heads. They knew it would never work, this mixed marriage. They are still shaking their heads – some dead, some alive – as they listen to Neela and Vikram arguing thirty years later.

The Thin Red Line

MODHURIMA SINHA

> 'The bonds of matrimony are like any other – they mature slowly.'
>
> —Peter De Vries

As a child I was always fascinated by the sindoor ceremony in Bengali weddings. There was always something so attractive about it. I suppose the colour red made it so gorgeous. But the strange part is that red never was my favourite colour. But red does stand out strikingly, very often drawing attention to the hidden. My fascination with the sindoor ceremony remains a mystery to me to this day, a bit ironic as I had discovered as a teenager that sindoor was symbolic of blood on the forehead of women being branded, as if they were part of herds traded. They were hit on the head, and the scar created remained, even after the blood dried up and the wound healed. The iron bangle worn by married women on the left hand is a symbol of shackles. Women it seems were always commodities.

Though the horror of these stories remained, I had not weaned myself off the fascination with sindoor. As a child I would wait for hours watching the ceremony – most of it, boring – till the end when the sindoor would be applied by the groom on the bride's forehead. It was like watching something reach completion.

Some weddings were agonies. States, languages, customs – we are further divided by caste, regions and more. So the Brahmins and Hindus from east Bengal had their sindoor ceremony known as '*kushondika*' the morning after the wedding. So all such weddings seemed incomplete to me, as we wouldn't be attending the morning ritual and the red splash would be missed. Maybe this excess ritualism made me into this hysterically anti-ritual person in my youth. I was an atheist, anti–all ceremonies, and was a minimalist.

When we were young intellectuals in Presidency College, there was a rage among many Bengali newly-weds to wear sindoor, starting from the tip of their noses. Whether it was done because of the colourful image it created, or of a desire to inform the world at large that they were married women, no longer innocent virgins, remains a mystery. We, the aspiring poets and literary analysts, were horrified at this non-intellectual fad. We generally looked down upon girls and women who wore sindoor. Nowadays, in all television serials – I have observed, fleetingly, while hunting for my news channel – sindoor is worn in abundance, sometimes as a flourish and sometimes as a dot.

I do not watch television serials as a rule, where women are mostly exaggerated, as either vamps or foolish victims, and are always overdressed. The discerning reader might wonder how I know these details, if I do not watch Indian soap. Well the truth is that at one point I tried watching a few, when recommended by people I knew. They were all without exception unbearable, and I never went beyond ten episodes, I think. I guess, once in a while one should know how bad it can get!

The marriage rituals are culturally interesting, but we as a nation are unable to detach ourselves from them. If we dealt with the ceremony just as an insignificant component, we would be happier trying to make a marriage work. But we keep going back to customs and rituals throughout our relationships. How elaborate the trousseau was, or how much jewellery was given, and by who, the dinner menus – all become a point of discussion, from which stem complaints, unhappiness, and extremities like dowry deaths.

In the twenty-first century we still make matches based on caste, creed and religion. The union of two people should be blessed because they want each other. There should never be any coercion. But from these rituals arise honour killings, where young couples are brutally murdered, mostly by their own parents and families.

The opposite of ritual is love. Or so I believe. No process or ritual can combat love. But force and violence can take over. So at the core of all marriages, which ideally love should rule, we may have disharmony. In India, we see how the interference of family members destroy marriages every day. The meaninglessness of all rituals is apparent when we see marriages breaking up, brides being killed, even after following all the detailed intricacies of them. Rituals cannot and do not hold marriages together. They are just symbolic.

Not all rituals are even respectable. The entire ceremony of kanyadaan can be really humiliating for any self-respecting woman. The father gives away the daughter to her husband. Why does she have to be given away? Because she is a commodity! She is not an individual, has no opinion, has no feelings, is like cattle.

Taking this further, the girl's mother cannot give her away, even if the father is dead or absconding. A male relative, an uncle, will then give the girl away. The woman is powerless – to give, to receive, to accept or to refuse. At the core of each ritual lies the denial of female agency. From being given away to being branded, it proves that a woman is a commodity.

There is another ritual by which the girl, on leaving her parents' home, throws back a handful of rice, saying, 'I am returning all my debts to you.' This is a singularly horrifying ritual, as it is impossible for any child to return her debt to parents, good or bad. The daughter is always indebted to her parents for having borne the trouble of bringing her up. She now goes to the home of her husband as a commodity to bear sons. Just a machine, really. The totally atrocious subjugation of the female form is about the only truth in the institution of marriage.

Love does not feature in the rituals. The man promises to look after and take care of the bride. There is a ceremony named *janmer bhaat kapor* where on the day of the *suhaag raat* (in Bengali families), the bride is handed a sari and a plateful of food as a symbol of taking care of her for life. In wealthy families, the bride is also given jewellery. So the promise is to feed, clothe and bejewel, but not to love, cherish and respect. Just maintenance! And originally they demanded maintenance fees, too, and to this very day they often still do – only the style has changed.

Marriage is the union, or is supposed to be, of two souls. The physical union which of course is also a ritual gives birth to children. The birth of a son! In the rat race for having sons, many forget that for birth to be possible, women are required.

Marriage allows a man to legally sleep with his wife. But making love and enjoying sex are not part of the ritual. It is an act of possession. Weirdly, even today, especially in urban India, many are grossly undereducated and think making love is something to be ashamed of and blush about. And often, the ritual of having sex, for the growth of progeny, is practised under coercion.

But in our country we make a ritual of almost anything. We have cultivated a ritual of rape now. Married or unmarried, women are getting raped every day, very often by gangs, and so many perpetrators go unpunished. The system rarely offers justice.

So it is with great respect that I treat all who dare break this ritualistic norm. When young couples, from different castes, classes, religions and communities, marry for love, there is cause to rejoice. When they face death and defy it all, foolish as it may seem, there is cause to rejoice. When same-sex couples marry, who would do the kanyadaan, and who is the kanya? Or who is the bride? All conventions are challenged – the system of possession and possessing. No wonder they are criminalized, for the lack of a solution.

Marriage in any case is a difficult institution, which rests on ground laid out on wobbly cobblestones. Most people do not realize that – ritual or no ritual, marriage is about adjusting. It is about two people learning to know each other, taking the best out of each other's book, and smoothening out the rough edges. Marriage is not dependent on any ritual at all. Marriage rituals are born out of the culture one is born into, like the food we eat is dependent on geography, the land where we live. So coastal cuisine includes fish and coconuts. In north India people eat less rice as rice is not grown there; the soil encourages wheat.

Many rituals of many communities are beautiful and have environmental and medicinal benefits. Like the haldi ceremony most Hindu weddings have. Turmeric is an antiseptic and has great benefits for the skin. If we could all have the rituals for their utilitarian and aesthetic value, life would be easier.

Marriage is not about a woman losing her identity but finding it. Why will I, as a recently married woman, change my food and sleep habits? The ideal marriage should have an exchange of values. And in impossible cases, which I do not want to dwell upon, the marriage should be cancelled.

Before I end, I have to admit that I did get married, and am still married. Almost twenty-three years! I was rebellious, so I did not want a ritual, did not want to invite a 1,000 people who would eat and then bitch in general. I wanted to invite about twenty people I liked. My father exploded and said I could do as I pleased. He would have to have a dinner in any case where about a 1,000 guests would be invited. Whether they were present or not that evening, he said he did not care. It was his duty – my father who was a forward-thinking, generous intellectual – he said, to feed people to whose homes he had been to over the years for various marriages. My to-be mother-in-law took great offence at my suggestion of a joint reception, since there were many common relations. As well-brought-up, educated youngsters we did not wish to annoy anybody. So, on my wedding day we had a 1,000 guests and my husband's family had another reception with 1,000 guests.

I did not allow most of the rituals and had a civil marriage. I avoided all the slapstick, which caused a few frowns. But I have to disclose that I did, in fact, insist on the sindoor ceremony! I never wore sindoor in real life, but couldn't resist my childhood obsession being enacted. (Was I mocking the system?) I felt like a hypocrite, but to this day I love my photographs with the red smudge on my forehead. It must be the artist, photographer and film-maker in me that loved that image. The visual appeal of that red is irresistible. But I am also embarrassed as a rational, thinking individual, and if there were a second life, I would marry with a few favourite people of mine, in the woods, or by the sea, just signing on a piece of paper if I had to.

The other secret I have to let out is that the same year during the pujas, on the last day of Durga Puja, which was at home, I indulged in sindoor khela, where married women apply sindoor on each other's forehead, in celebration, after putting sindoor on the icon of Durga. In a nation where we worship the female powers, in a nation where brides are burnt to death, in a country where the girl child is murdered every day – we live in a mire of contradictions.

Marriage in any relationship needs sharing and tolerance; there are differences; but there are agreements too; space ought to be given to fulfil individual needs and desires, giving rise to new ideas and forms and intimate moments of belonging that make life meaningful. Marriage can be between any two people of any age, any sex, any caste, any class, as long as it is consensual.

And the rituals have no role to play in it. So what if I did indulge in a bit of sindoor khela...?

A Girl of a Certain Age

Abha Iyengar

> 'The world, in its best state, is nothing more than a larger assembly of beings, combining to counterfeit happiness which they do not feel, employing every art and contrivance to embellish life, and to hide their real condition from the eyes of one another.'
>
> —Samuel Johnson, *The Adventurer*, No. 120, December 1753

'Happily married' is a state everyone says they are in once they are married. Very few women will own up to the kind of compromises they are forced to make after marriage, or even at the time of choosing a groom for themselves – rather, even at the time a groom *is* chosen for them.

In our lives, we talk of relationships and their importance, and of course, marriage is one such exalted relationship. Exalted because for a girl in India, however accomplished she may be or advanced in her career, everything will just take second place to marriage. There may be a very small percentage of women who overcome this social construct. The Indian social set-up requires that one get 'settled' at a certain age. And being settled means to be married and thereafter have children. And if you, as a girl, are married as soon as you turn eighteen, no one will raise an eyebrow; but if you remain unmarried beyond twenty-seven ... well then, heaven help you.

There will be talk about not getting the eligible guys (already booked), the biological clock-ticking, losing the youthful look, not being young enough to 'adjust' as required, the unwillingness to give up career if required, the friends who have married and left you behind, and being a burden on the parents who have done so much to bring you up ... the list is endless and deafening in its clamour.

Once upon a time there was this young, beautiful, smart, intelligent and witty girl...

This is the story of a young, fun-loving Stephanian who had all the boys running after her, who was propositioned left, right and centre.

But she didn't want any of them, her heart given to a guy she was so crazy over that she would spend as much time as possible as she could with him. She wanted to marry him and it seemed, as fairytales go, he wanted to marry her as well. However, he was the same age as her, a young college-going boy, with no earnings of his own. Meanwhile, the girl's father began to talk marriage to her, for she had completed her graduation, and was now ready to be married off. Further studies for this one-time Commonwealth topper could happen after marriage, if she so desired ... as though marriage were a crystal ball through which all dreams could come true.

So the boy was asked by the girl's father, 'Do you wish to marry her?'

'Yes,' he said, 'but not now. I have to become independent first.'

'But you can marry her. She can live with you and your parents, the family is well known and established.'

The boy said, 'The family will not agree, and … I cannot go against their wishes.'

This girl, a twenty-year-old fresh out of college, from a respectable family and having received a great education and upbringing, was at the boy's feet, clinging and imploring and asking, 'But … why can't you marry me? Please, marry me, J…'

You would think a scene like this happens in a back-of-beyond place like Jhumri Telaiyan, but this was happening in an urban household, and the scene was not from some Bollywood tearjerker where the girl is to fall at the boy's feet and beg for marriage. This was Delhi, this was the late '70s, this was the Age of Freedom, and this was happening in a house where one was given several liberties and opportunities.

'J' pushed her away, very much like they do in films, and said, 'I am too young for this. My parents won't approve.' And he turned on his heel, walked out the house, and did not connect with her again. Thus ended what was supposed to be a fairytale.

The girl who had been at the boy's feet, at our home, was my sister.

Watching this scene unfold before my eyes destroyed me. My marriage had been fixed and I was to be married the following month. Meanwhile, I was studying for an exam I would sit for post marriage, even as I felt the ground slip from under my feet. A sense of being unwanted had begun to prevail over me, something I had not felt before, of being suddenly pushed away. And here was my sister, younger to me by a year and a half, next in line and already being prepared for marriage, for what would prove to be a noose around her neck.

My father began to arrange for rishtas for her. His unreasonable reasoning was that her broken heart would be healed and her problems solved ... by the next man in her life. This man would come into her life through an arranged marriage. However, my heartbroken sister, emotionally crushed, kept saying no to all the proposals that came her way.

While a string of men followed one another, I saw her retreating into herself, becoming a shadow of who she was. My parents did not understand what was happening. They had an arranged marriage and had made their adjustments without any qualms. All I can say is it is a good thing they had not emotionally given themselves to anyone else. Or it could be that my sister was just that much more emotionally vulnerable. I would say that she just did not get enough time to recover from a broken heart, a broken sense of self.

The question my father, reeling under his own frustrations of not having things going as per plan before he retired, asked her, after she kept saying no, was, 'So what's so great about you that you keep saying no to all the men?'

She spiralled downwards, and my parents realized she was in the throes of deep depression. Doctors were consulted and medicines given. And, finally, a marriage was arranged. The boy was Indian, residing in Canada.

Tunnel Vision

'I love you,' she said.

She lay there on the bed, dressed to meet the groom-to-be.

Her eyes were wide open, her red lips a slash across her face. The smile did not reach her eyes, which looked vacant. Dead.

If you looked close enough...

He looked close enough, looking down as he was on her, lying there on the bed.

Didn't it strike him as funny that she, a young girl of twenty, should be lying down and receiving him in the bedroom?

Perhaps it was the done thing after all.

'I love you, too,' he said. He was meeting her for the first time.

The meeting had been arranged by the respective parents.

Her parents, looking on, hiding their anxiety, smiled.

'They love each other.' They nodded to each other. This was indeed a blessed union.

She would soon forget her previous lover; her depression would disappear; marriage was 'the solution'.

He left.

She got out of bed. She would dance throughout the night. The drugs would do the rest.

A painted rag doll.

I sobbed quietly.

My beautiful sister. Slithering in a dark tunnel not of her making.

This is the first piece of flash fiction I wrote and it was published online in Insolent Rudder (2004). The editor called the story 'visceral'. What else can something like this be, that tears you apart as an unpalatable truth?

The make-believe perfect world of marriage does not exist. For some it works out better, for most it is compromise, different forms of it. So why is it made out to be the only and ultimate aim for a woman to aspire to?

Manju Kapur in her first novel *Difficult Daughters* (Penguin Books, 1998), which won the Commonwealth Writers for the Eurasian Region (1999), traces the lot of Indian women from pre-Partition days to the present through three generations of women of a family from Amritsar. Ida is the third-generation narrator in this novel who tries to find her sense of self through exploring her mother Virmati's life story. Virmati, born in 1940, is seventeen years old at the time she fails her FA (school) exams. She protests to her mother, Kasturi, that the demands of the joint family, which involves taking care of her siblings, have sabotaged her studies. Kasturi finds her daughter's disappointment and protests unreasonable. She believes it hardly makes a difference to the real business of her daughter's life, 'which was getting married and looking after her own home'. The concept of marriage and taking care of a family has been ingrained in the Indian woman's being so much that a divorced Ida, even though considering herself to be free, finds herself 'hovering like a pencil notation on the margins of society'.

One can say, times have changed since the '70s and the '90s, and we are now near completing two decades of the twenty-first century. Perceptions and people have changed, and women do not consider marriage to be the ultimate destination, nor do families. Girls are more independent and outspoken. They no longer toe the line.

However, for a majority of young women, the age limit may have gone up from twenty-one to twenty-seven over the years, but after that, parents still get nervous and begin to apply pressure on the girl to 'settle down' which means 'get married'.

One of my daughter's friends told her how, now that she was twenty-seven, her parents wished to find a boy for her to get married to, and so she needed to

(a) stop partying so much,
(b) start coming home by 11 p.m. and not 3 a.m. when she did party,
(c) begin dressing more carefully – nothing too short, nothing too low.

This is how it begins. One can only wonder why her parents granted her these freedoms in the first place. Were they pretending to be 'modern'? And had they granted her all this only to slam it all away when she reached a certain age? And why should she now have to pretend to be different than what she is? Start leading a more restricted life that's not her choice? I believe the standard advertisement call for the bride to be a 'homely, comely, smart and educated girl' hasn't changed an iota over the years. What has changed is that the girl may now do the household work and also contribute to the household kitty, with often no control on the funds she earns.

Recently, Manjula Chakravorty,* a twenty-eight-year-old professional, said that she had to get married at the earliest to *relieve her parents of her burden*. She actually said she 'understood' that she was a burden to her parents.

She is the eldest of two kids, with a brother a couple of years younger. It appears that in no way is he considered a 'burden'. This girl is a postgraduate, has studied in London, lives away from her parents (who reside in Ghaziabad), in a south Delhi apartment and works in the corporate sector. Yet, she is willing to get married to one of the various men her parents will list for her to choose from, vetting them on some parameters like age, education, status, salary, family background, etc. Nothing is known of the emotional quotient here. It's a matter of luck, a toss of the coin, that she will find someone who is compatible. All said and done, marriages are supposedly made in heaven, so the man should be just right for her. And if it does not turn out fine, the girl had better lump it to save her parents' face or nose, which they usually prize more than their daughter's well-being or sanity.

Girls kill their ambitions to conform, to get married and to remain married. Ujaala Sachdeva wanted to become a chef in a

---

*Names have been changed

five-star hotel and had the opportunity to do so. Married some two years ago, she now delivers cakes and breads from home to clients because the family requires that she work from home. By family, one means in-laws, because she doesn't have children yet. She could have chosen 'not to get married and live her life', but she toed the line, for at twenty-five she was 'of marriageable age'. This was a love marriage and the man she married was of her choice, but, talking to her, you know that she is unhappy she was given no choice in continuing her work where and how she wanted. She has been compelled to stifle a part of herself.

Twenty-seven-year-old Chandrika Choudhary says, '"I am a good girl", (is what) I kept telling myself for almost two point five decades of my life until it started to suffocate me as (after this) I could not justify it any more! What was I doing wrong, after the perfect academic record, a dream job, sustaining myself independently in the capital city, no habits that the society would disapprove of, and travelling extensively? What could go against my "good girl" tag? Well, I had turned twenty-six and was unmarried and been refusing a few proposals that I thought were not right for me.

'I went home to spend my twenty-sixth birthday with my parents but ended up crying most of the time because my dad would not talk to me as I was in disagreement to marry the second guy (shown to me), who kept asking me about the compromises I would make after marriage, changing my job and several other questions that at that point made me think, How *claustrophobic* it is to be in marriage?'

Chandrika belongs to a small town of UP. She said she owes a lot to her parents, especially her father, who did not stop or question her when she was rampantly switching subjects to finally complete a master's in adventure tourism. Working with a European tourism board for the past five years, she has had a chance to see the world, sometimes just solo with her backpack! She was never questioned nor stopped by her parents even when she planned a trek for nine days without a phone in Kashmir or in the landslide-prone area of Uttarakhand, or spent a night at a railway station in Austria! Her father 'empowered' her and it was due to her parents' trust and composure that she could do all these with ease.

However, she says, 'I still sometimes feel like a walking disgrace when I am in front of my extended family. I look at people and imagine them silently talking to me, and asking, "Why are you not getting married? What is wrong with you?" They think that excessive education/exposure has ruined me. In the last three years, I have been asked varied questions on my orientation, my take on marriage, if I am dating someone who is not yet ready or if I really want to settle down. I have walked into hospitals and funerals to have people fixing me with someone. *Sadly, no one asked me what I wanted*. It was always what they thought could be a right fix. It hurts to know that people don't understand – a man with decent income, family and career is not always a choice. In this age, we have been nurtured to fight for our dreams, choices, college, hobbies, etc. How can I just go ahead and plan to have kids with a man I am not even attracted to!'

About a year and half ago, Chandrika was really depressed. 'Not because I couldn't find a man to marry but because of the unhappiness the whole thing brought to my parents; it strained my relationship with them. I reduced calls and visits to home, as anything more than five minutes would end up with, "*Aaj koi mila? Dekha koi?*" (Did you find anyone today? See anyone?)

'I started playing hide-and-seek with my parents, took up travel, especially to locations with limited coverage. That was my cooling-off period! At one point, I would cry often and really wished, if it had to come, death would come now; at least I would die happily, without having to live with some guy forcefully ... I tried to talk to so many people, relate to each, find help through religious and spiritual means. In the last three years, I have done so many religious remedies, just for the sake of my parents.

'I have been listed on and off on all matrimonial websites, newspapers, and anything else you can think of! I sincerely made an effort to go ahead and try. My last attempt, apart from secretly making my own account on shaadi.com, was a "speed meet" event, where I met about ten guys in an hour, for five minutes each. Let's say it didn't go well; after the event, four of us girls went out cribbing and had a similar story (we were all aged twenty-five to twenty-eight). I was relaxed to know I was not sailing through the storm alone!

'Nonetheless, *I still feel I am the pending responsibility my parents quickly want to get over with*, so much so that they have made me meet guys I would never even talk (to) even if they were sitting next to me in a train.

'I still haven't conveyed the idea to parents, that things are no longer the same in my head, and I won't just accept someone with compromises until I am convinced about the person.'

Chandrika does want to get married, but she says, 'My future plan is to keep looking out while I keep myself engaged with my hobbies and make plans for life without having deadlines of marriage in my head. I have to keep motivating myself amidst all the pressure.'

Chandrika gives one hope, largely because she has not caved in, and is still trying to find a way out for herself. She admits: 'A conversation is due with my parents. I know it will blow up things for a while, but I can't drag myself with a burden every day! I have started to enjoy life again and am trying to rekindle my relationship with parents with a belief that when the time is right I will find a life partner.'

The idea of marriage is a very complicated one. It is such a great change for any person to experience, and there are no hard-and-fast guidelines for making it work, because two individuals who have till now led separate lives and with different family set-ups, with different existing equations, now need to forge a new understanding between them.

For most women, it is a forced equation, where the woman has to make all the required adjustments. *Lipstick under My Burqa*, the film by Alankrita Shrivastava (through the character of Shireen played by Konkona Sen Sharma) brings home the fact that even in 2017, marriage can suffocate and deny choice and freedom. Many women, post marriage, have little or no control over their bodies, their relationships, family life or career decisions. To be pushed into a marriage by parents who consider the girl a burden to be got rid of after a certain time … is a kind of murder, the murder of an individual's choice.

The concept of marriage, as the ultimate goal for a woman to work towards for her own happiness, must change. A girl should not be considered by parents to be a 'burden' to be disposed off, or a 'task' to be ticked off from a to-do list. A woman should go ahead and make an informed choice regarding the life she wants for herself. Chandrika's parents have to truly 'empower' themselves and their daughter by letting her be and not push her into marriage. My sister fell headlong over a precipice … It was a situation where she had no control. In Chandrika's case, as in the case of all women of today, the decision regarding their marriage should lie with them.

In most countries, marriage is becoming a redundant institution. It may take quite some time for this to happen in India, but while it is alive, it should not be made into a heaven to be aimed for at any cost. Girls should be taught different; taught to reach for the moon, and not the man; taught that they are treasures and not tasks.

Across Latitudes and Longitudes

WENDELL RODRICKS

It is 5 a.m. at Goa airport. The Qatar Airways flight is delayed for over an hour and I wonder if I will make the connection to Chicago from Doha. A zombie line makes its way to the aircraft as the tedious boarding begins. Up on the Dabolim plateau, a chilly wind sweeps across the vast grassland. I huddle deeper into pashmina wool.

As the doors shut with a whispering whoosh, I glance at the blonde lady in an all grey ensemble. She is ready for the chill in her hometown. Her parka takes its own time to get into the overhead rack. The lady's demeanour is as sombre as mine. The sun bursts into a glowing ball over the Arabian Sea as the plane shudders to take off.

Six a.m. and champagne on offer? What the hell! This is going to be a long journey. Might as well celebrate the journey and the holiday ahead. My neighbour accepts a flute too. Then we do the decent thing which utter strangers indulge in, rather frequently, when thrown together in confined pressurized air spaces.

'Cheers!'

We clink glasses with the direct eye contact all Europeans toast with (or suffer seven years of bad sex, they claim), when I notice a tear well up in the blue-grey left eye and slide slow-motion-like into the straw-coloured bubbles.

I offer a napkin. Some sniffles later, and at a loss for words, I simply say 'I'm sorry'. For what, I do not know. An accident in Goa. A holiday gone bad. A loved one at death's door at home. An already departed soul into the ether?

Instead, what is offered as the reason is closer to my heart. As the plane wings westwards and upwards, longitude by latitude, Helga tells me about her tears. With a distant look in her eyes ... over a spinach-filled, fluffy omelette.

She is in love with a Goan man whom she met in Germany. She came to Goa to meet him for two weeks. All too short. He could not get another Schengen visa so quickly. And she cannot marry him immediately because the procedure would take its own time.

After a sencha green tea, I watch as she falls into a deep, sad slumber.

I look out of the window at the vast ocean sparkling with sequins. Soon we will cross the Musandam with its ragged, sky-piercing peaks and choppy waters skimming at the white sand-beach edges, like layers of shaded georgette that morph from pale turquoise to deep cobalt.

It was down this Omani coast, thirty years ago, that I had gone for a walk in the moonlight with a stranger. A Frenchman who would become my partner, friend and love. For three decades, the biggest challenge was not the clash of Oriental and Occidental cultures – there were many moments of those, under scrutiny from two curious, initially disapproving, then totally embracing, mafia-type families. Sublime moments when

Goan fiery vindaloo forcibly met chilled raw Brittany oysters; when Old Monk rum competed with Rhum Agricole from the French West Indies; when Indian kurtas met Yves Saint Laurent couture. When Cartier sat alongside Ganjam jewels. When strange misinterpretations of foreign languages shocked new in-laws: when I translated, post a heavy meal, 'I am stuffed', from Catering College menu lingo, into '*Je suis farci*' ('I am fucked' in French). When he said he was 'angry' and I wondered what I had done. He was merely 'hungry' ... with a French accent.

On it went. Indian hospitality for my parents meant an air ticket went with an invitation to visit Europe. French practicality insisted that his parents pay their way to India and Goa (Indianess won the round and the French parents did fly on gifted tickets).

In the end one learns to balance. Salad and French fare for lunch, Indian fusion for dinner. Seating people for dinner à la Française with 'placement' ... one girl, one boy, main guest on the right of the hosts, etc., for meals that went on for three hours... versus Indian parties where people drink for three hours and dine at a buffet in ten minutes, and then leave 'ta ta' ... not to unwind over cigars and cognac/liqueurs for a further hour or two.

There was always one fly in the ointment of our togetherness. Actually make that two annoying flies. Latitude and longitude. Those irritating lines and borders between countries. Why did they not simply follow what John Lennon sang in 'Imagine'?

Heterosexuals have it so easy. They get married, they have a paper that can get them a spouse's country's passport or a PIO or OCI. I see some of my models. They bonk a 'phirangi', marry him and then next day he gets valid Indian resident status.

How can one write in a visa form under 'Reason for Visit' ... love?

Yes 'love', you moron immigration systems. A love between one man and another. So no Angola for me. I had to stew in

Paris. And the Turkish guys wanted to know why I should get a multiple-entry annual visa. How about love again! But I couldn't write that. Gay is taboo topic.

This was becoming a battle zone. Even after twenty-one years together, we were standing in different immigration lines. He would be out in a flash. I would be at Athens airport, thrown in a room with illegal immigrants even though I had a valid visa. After much yelling I would get victory. Or in the Maldives, I would get singled out for an HIV blood sample test. Excusez moi? Or in Sydney, a 'random explosives test'. It was always 'random'. I have got thick-skinned about racism with age.

I hated now three lines on the planet. Latitudes, longitudes and borders.

Somehow love survived.

With plotting and planning, India and Goa became home. I signed a French PACS in 2002. Never stood in a separate immigration queue again. Unless it was Kenya or Senegal where you are thrown in jail and killed for loving someone of the same sex. In such countries (hello Putin's Russia) we stand in different lines on purpose.

More jubilation followed on 2 July 2001 when the Delhi High Court did not frown at 'unnatural sex' as criminal. I lit candles and prayed for judges Muralidhar and Shah at the local shrine, blessing them for their wisdom and Nehruvian philosophy of inclusiveness for all citizens in India.

At long last, I felt we were winning the battle of the 'lines'. Those torturous lines were being erased. I felt a part of this beloved country. Dignity had been restored. It was exhilarating, liberating … this taste of freedom. Then a dark cloud unleashed a terrible storm in 2013.

The war was no more against latitudes and longitudes. The Supreme Court of India had us in their crosshairs. In one sweep of deplorable, unfair judgment, some fifty million to possibly ninety million LGBT people were labelled 'criminals'.

We are still in the latitude and longitude battle. In a country as vast as India, the lines continue to haunt, terrorize and induce fear. Is this fair to the future generations? I will battle the lines again. From the front line. I must. How can I not – a future generation wants us to soldier on. For love, for them. To save them from clandestine parks and public toilets. From sad marriages made for social appearances. From a life of oppression.

The captain announces the scheduled landing in Doha. Stewardesses offer a round of refreshments. I turn to Helga and offer her a copy of my memoir, *The Green Room*.

'Your love will survive borders. You are straight. You will marry and settle in Germany or Goa. But say a prayer for us. We are a love doomed to live between the lines. Beyond the lines. In the shadows. It is time to ring in freedom. Hopefully it will come in my lifetime.'

It is now my turn to let a tear drop ... into nothingness!

What I Hate Most

Milan Vohra

I hate that because of her I failed my final-year exams in college. The study table in my room was unfortunately positioned in a way that gave me an excellent view into the next house. Into a strategic part of her bedroom. The corner that served as both dressing room and undressing room. I use the word unfortunate because it pushed my life in a direction I hadn't planned.

I hate how all his life he's blamed what he does, which is run a business, neither big nor small, just a very high-on-headache and low-on-profits business of running a small fancy lights showroom, on meeting me. If he'd spent the last few months of his BCom actually looking into his books and not at the *Playboy* magazines he always hid inside his books, and definitely not peering through the crack in the curtains of my bedroom, he could have been whatever he wanted. A professional at least.

I hate that she has always been so partial to red. Always turning this way and that, preening before that mirror, flaunting those buxom curves, those wide hips in her tight red satiny kurtas, every line in her body shining, catching the light, reeling me in.

I hate that he has always justified and made excuses for his own weakness for dusky skin. Especially dusky skin in red. It was me, he said, and the conniving of my mother which was responsible for trapping him so early in a marriage. When the truth is he couldn't have been happier when his father found my photos hidden inside each of his books and insisted that he start a business and get married straight away.

I hate that even in the throes of passion, in the days that it used to happen, her awe-inspiring thighs could be wrapped around my waist, squeezing me, eyes shut tight, yet still she could continue talking. Silence: The woman doesn't know what it means.

I hate that in all the twenty-nine years we have been married he is always simultaneously reading a newspaper and listening to me, or looking at his account books and listening to me, or watching his stupid cricket and refilling his drink and listening to me ... sometimes I wonder if he is only pretending to listen to me. The only time I can get his undivided attention is when he is in bed with me. And then he complains that I don't have anything interesting to say to him. Well, you tell me – when do I fit in talking about other important things like what wedding gift to send his cousin sister or when he plans to fix the broken flush?

I hate how she keeps asking me to do idiotic jobs that she thinks a man should do, when she and I both know I can leave the shop only after I've checked everything – the petty cash, getting the boys to lock up – and thus reach home only at 8.30 or 9 p.m. every night. We both know who is going to take care of these things and I don't think it's too much to ask from her for the life of leisure she has.

I hate that he thinks I do nothing, absolutely nothing with my day except sit on the phone or go shopping in malls with my friends. Who went and took his father for physiotherapy every day for months on end? Who devoted hours to his sister and got her out of her depression when her husband wanted that divorce? Who attended every single marriage, every single death ceremony for every single distant relation on his side of the family, too? Left to him, we would have no contact with society at all. All he wants is to just come back home and sit in front of the TV, day after day, never go out anywhere. Not even for soup to a Chinese restaurant.

I hate that she asks me the same question every single year, just around our anniversary time. 'Do you love me?' Is that something to wonder about, when you have shared the same bed every night, night after night, even through the times she had declared a cold war. It's all because of these romances she keeps reading.

I hate how even today it hurts, because like a fool I want him to say something different, something from his heart just once to me. But every time, once in the year when I tell myself I'll ask him once more, just this last time, 'Do you love me?', he looks surprised as if it's so immature of me to want to know. 'What kind of silly question is that?' That's his answer. Every single year.

I hate to say this, but it still amazes me that, mentally, she really hasn't grown out of her teens. The way she can leave thousands of clothes all over the bedroom floor, the bathroom floor – this before we go to a party. It's not as if we go out that often. You'd think she could have planned what she will wear a little in advance.

I hate – really, really hate – how he has an opinion on any and every thing I wear. It's the double standard, really, that bothers me. I can go to so much trouble to get a new blouse made to wear for a function, with the latest deep-cut sleeveless style, but he will bluntly tell me that women with heavy arms should not wear sleeveless clothes.

I hate that she doesn't understand I know men better. I know what is really in their minds when a woman with satiny skin is ready to show it to the world.

I hate the way he says he hates socializing, and then can readily spend hours charming and flattering that horrible witch of a woman, Vimla or *Vimlaji* as she likes to be called, admiring her spaghetti-string blouse.

I hate that she is so insecure. I only have to speak to somebody, and God forbid it should be a woman. Before I know it, the cold war is upon me. Weeks upon weeks of silent tea, silent laying out of clothes on the bed, silent relaying of messages from the family, silent job lists and updates on plumbers and electricians, silent sex. Although the last one, I suppose I don't actually completely hate. But I do hate that she won't even make the soft sighs and sounds she does when I do the things she likes to her.

I hate that he never even tries to think of a gift to give me for our anniversary. Just because I wanted to change the sari he bought for me once. Now, it's always that white envelope. The amount inside has changed and yes, I agree he's never been stingy with me. But for once in our life can't he try to think of something I would really like? I tell him, what are you, seventy-five or something? Come on, loosen up, sell the shop, the business; let's go on a foreign trip.

I hate that she thinks the only way she will see the world is if I sell my shop and then take her on that trip. Maybe it's good she doesn't understand finance and hasn't caught on about the loan I've been working on. This will be the first big gift I am getting for her in our life. Two tickets to Thailand. For our thirtieth anniversary. I hate that she thinks it's boring when I try to explain our finances to her. Or explain what papers are in which file. Yes, I know I'm being morbid to talk of wills when I'm fifty-five but someone has to be an adult here.

I hate that I hate the smell of hospitals and that it is the one thing I cannot bring myself to do – I just cannot get myself to sleep a night inside one. I suppose I have to admit he's saved me that nightmare when my mother had her surgeries. Each and every one of them. God bless her soul.

I hate that she thinks it's not important to tell me where she's going. She gets touchy when I tell her to stop driving that antique scooter of hers.

I hate that he insists on treating me like a child. It's as if it is to compensate for the one we almost had but then lost. I hate it when my friends tease me, 'You two; you have to report to each other every hour or what?' I sometimes delay calling him back the moment I see his missed call just to get him used to not having me drop whatever I'm doing to instantly speak to him.

I hate the way the traffic has gone totally out of control in this city. I hate to admit it but maybe he's right. Maybe I need to get myself a second-hand car. At least then I won't have to try to pull up to the side of the road every time it rains.

I hate that she won't answer her phone.

I hate that he calls me on the dot of the hour every hour. Come rain or shine. Especially in this rain.

I hate that she doesn't understand; if she doesn't answer, I worry.

I hate that he doesn't understand it's not possible to answer every call. I hate how slippery these roads are.

I hate this ringtone she has. '*Kaho na pyaar hai*.' I hate how it stops right in the middle of the word 'pyaar' and then that irritating recorded voice tells you the number you are trying to reach is not responding. I know that. Damn it. I know.

I hate the way somehow I can see the red, the bright shining red seeping under me, merging with the rain water, yet it is somehow a thing apart, that intense shade of blood, surrounding me, wrapping itself over me, draping my clothes, my skin, highlighting, hugging closely each abundant curve of my body the way my red satin kurtas did. The ones he used to say made him fall in love with me.

I hate the realization as it slowly occurs to me, as I sit stunned beside her, that I will never be able to tell her. This one year, I had finally thought of a different reply; when she would invariably ask, 'Do you love me?', I thought I would say 'What kind of a silly question is that? Why do you want words for everything?' And then I would give it to her. In my pocket, the envelope with the tickets inside. The first real gift that I was confident she would not want to change. For our thirtieth anniversary tomorrow.

What I hate most of all is the deafening silence of the ambulance siren as it negotiates its way to hospital. The silence from her fills my heart like thick cotton plugged into my ears. I tell myself she's doing it again. That cold war thing she loves to torture me with. And look, she's doing it again. Flaunting that vivid red she's always been so partial to. Sticky and warm. On her. On me. Still falling to the ground as she is rushed into EMERGENCY. All the life drained out of her. And me.

Sacrament, Contract or Relationship?

Vijay Nagaswami

As a keen observer of the Indian marriage for close on three decades, and having been provided the unique opportunity to participate professionally in the distinctively complex issues that Indian married couples have had to struggle with, I am uniquely placed to appreciate that though making generalizations about Indian marriages is a perilous undertaking, at least two can still be made.

The first of these is that despite the increasing marital turbulence that young urban Indians now experience, and despite the consequent increase in divorce rates, the only industry that doesn't seem to feel the impact of the global recession is the wedding industry in our country, for we remain a nation obsessed with marriage. The second of these is that the contemporary Indian marriage looks, at least on the surface, appreciably different from the marriage of a couple of decades ago, since social change in urban India during this period has, against conventional sociological wisdom, taken place at a galloping pace, ushering in what I refer to as the New Indian Marriage.

From even a cursory scan of the global literature on marriage through the ages, it becomes readily apparent that marriage was essentially conceived of as a space to give protection and legitimacy to the procreated progeny of a man and a woman. Marriage was preceded by 'pair-bonding', wherein a man and a woman decided, in their respective mutual interests, to spend some portion of their lifetimes together, under the watchful eyes of the tribal leadership to ensure that neither partner abdicated their responsibilities to their offspring. Monogamy was not necessarily considered an inherent aspect of marriage. But as tribes grew and migration occurred, the need for social codes was experienced by ancient societies.

At that time, marriage was an unwritten contract of convenience that could still be enforced by the community leadership, since the number of people were still small. With the passage of time, marriage became an instrument of expansion of family, and tribal wealth and influence, and eventually became popular with royalty, to contract alliances and expand territories. Probably the first recorded marriage contracts were around 4,000 years ago in Mesopotamia, which formally ushered in the conceptualization of marriage as a 'contract' between two people, two families, two tribes and often two kingdoms.

With the ascendance of organized religion, the issue of morality entered the domain of marriage and, as a result, it soon came to be viewed as a 'sacrament', solemnized in the presence of God; a bond that could never be severed, regardless of situations and circumstances. The need to create an institution around 'pair-bonding' arose against the background of the institution of the family, largely to create, protect and legitimize 'bloodlines'. Later, with the emergence of the notion of 'ownership' of property, the need to institutionalize marriage was even more keenly felt and this resulted in the involvement of the State in marriage. As a result, over the last couple of centuries or so, marriage laws came into existence replacing hitherto idiosyncratic 'conventions' that had been difficult, if not impossible, to implement uniformly.

At the time, since marriages were by and large alliances contracted by families looking to enhance their genetic purity, social standing and wealth, the institution of marriage operated principally on the values of duty, responsibility and procreation (not unlike the situation in many parts of our country even today). Marriage, however, continued to operate under the broader umbrella of patriarchy since men were the dominant gender in both religious orders as well as the State.

It was only in the second half of the nineteenth century or so that the issue of 'love' entered the institution of marriage, and marriages came to be considered as relationships of love, companionship and emotional intimacy, under the ostensibly benign sanction of religion and State, as long as such relationships observed some basic rules and disciplines ordained by both these institutions.

In our country, marriage has been, and in some parts continues to be, dictated by the *Manusmriti* (Laws of Manu) which were arguably written more than three and a half millennia ago. As a result, marriage has always been considered a sacrament by Hindus. Muslims, Christians and subscribers to other religions in the country too tend to view marriage as a sacrament, some also as a contract. And since we are a religiously pluralistic nation, the Indian marriage is governed by a plethora of legislations, each specific to the different religious groups in the country, although all of them have some common elements, especially when it comes to the dissolution of marriage. However, over the last two decades or so, the perception of and approach to marriage has changed in urban, educated India. The New Indian Marriage cannot any more be viewed purely as a sacrament. Or as a contract. Or even as a relationship. It's a bit of this, some of that and more of the other.

But, before exploring the phenomenon of the New Indian Marriage, let us take a look at the 'New Indian', a recently emerging metropolitan creature who is perfectly happy to live in India, despite its warts. Even if an overseas work assignment is sought it is more for the experience, the independence away from the family and for enhancing the résumé than for leaving the homeland for good. Apparently, the grass is green enough on this side. Paav bhaji and masala dosa are as much enjoyed as pizzas and hamburgers; Kumbakonam degree coffee as much as cappuccino; tender coconut water as much as energy drinks; Shahrukh Khan as much as George Clooney; the salsa as much as the garba; Art of Living as much as Stephen Covey. In other words, the New Indian does not reject India and Indian. Other things from other parts of the world just get added on. The New Indian's patriotism is not of the jingoistic, chest-beating variety. Being an Indian is just a fact of life. It's who she or he is. It doesn't need to be cried out from the rooftops, nor does it need to be a well-guarded secret.

The New Indian is more pan-Indian in perspective, perhaps on account of leading a more mobile life. Born in Ludhiana, educated in Kolkata, MBA from Lucknow, working in Chennai and married to a Gujarati is no longer an exceptional scenario. The New Indian does not make a big deal of language; it is seen more as a tool for communication than as a definer of identity. The New Indian tends to live life more consciously. As a result, relationships are more emotionally intense and personal experiences more meaningful. However, the New Indian is also impatient, brash and in-your-face. Frustration tolerance is poor. Instant gratification is demanded and the tendency towards impulsive decision-making is strongly evident. Political awareness and participation is not particularly high on the New Indian's agenda, except over the last year or so. Art is not as highly valued as is entertainment. And the risk of conspicuous consumption also looms.

All of these attributes of the New Indian find reflection in the New Indian Marriage, which is no longer seen as an inevitable stage of life, but as a life domain that needs to be nurtured and configured to provide emotional fulfilment. Put differently, the New Indian Marriage is slowly growing into a distinctive entity that is far more consciously experienced than it ever used to be. The fact that divorce rates are on the increase need not be cause for concern, for re-marriage rates are still fairly high (we are, as I began by saying, a nation obsessed with marriage).

Although the meaning of marriage to younger couples is perceptibly different from that of their parents, when one scratches the surface of the New Indian Marriage, the differences in content may not be too startling, for the dynamics of the Indian family has not changed overly. This is really the greatest source of conflict that emerge in many contemporary marriages, for young people who are taking a shot at modernity may still be bound by some vestigial bonds of tradition that remain firmly entrenched in their minds, even though they may not be conscious of them.

The differences between the Old and New Indian Marriage begin to make their appearance right from the point of partner choice. I recently came across a statistic verified by UNICEF, Human Rights Commission and ABC News that about 90 per cent of Indian marriages are arranged. Although I am just guessing – since there is no organized data on the subject – the rate of arranged marriages in urban, educated India may be slightly lower than this. However, there can be no doubt that even in this population, arranged marriages are far more likely to be the norm than marriages of choice. Most arranged marriages start off as a sacrament, since this is what binds two relative strangers to each other. However, within a year or so, the difference between this form of marriage and its opposite number, the 'love marriage' (an odious term, really), starts getting blurry, for most young urban Indians, regardless of the manner of partner selection, seem to have similar expectations of marriage – a companionable, intimate and expressively loving relationship that doesn't violate or offend the rest of the family, particularly the parents. Not, by any stretch of imagination, identical to the stoical and fatalistic manner with which their parents approached the whole business of marriage.

Aside from the two broad patterns of partner choice – 'arranged' and 'love' marriages – a couple of new ones seem to have emerged. As a young, recently married designer (what precisely she designed was never quite clear) explained to me, she allowed her marriage to be arranged only to get her parents off her back and because she couldn't find a suitable boy for herself. However, she had made it clear to her parents that while they could shortlist the boys for her, she'd marry only someone she fell in love with. She did so with the eighth boy she 'saw' and he, on his part, reciprocated her feelings for him. They had an 'arranged-cum-love' marriage, she said, obviously pleased with herself for categorizing their marriage so impeccably. Her implication in including a 'love' component to her marriage was to underscore the point that both of them were looking for more from the marriage than those who entered a 'traditional arranged' marriage. Duty, responsibility and role-playing were to be replaced by love, companionship and intimacy. And in truth, these were the values that dominated their marriage.

In what has, in recent times, come to be called a 'love-cum-arranged' marriage, which just means that both partners fell in love with each other before deciding to get married, and their respective parents were perfectly happy to go along, or were persuaded to do so, the family takes over once the partner choice is made, and their continuing involvement in the couple's life means that the marriage becomes pretty much indistinguishable from an arranged marriage. In such a marriage, since both partners are 'grateful' to their respective parents for 'allowing' them to go ahead with their chosen partners, they tend to bend over backwards to please their parents, who end up playing stellar roles in their children's marriage.

In essence, the most palpable hallmark of the New Indian Marriage is the issue of 'ownership' of the marriage. As can be seen from the foregoing passages, there appears to be a need to juxtapose a component of 'love' into the very nomenclature of the 'arranged marriage'. It would be easy to dismiss this as a shallow attempt at pursuing modernity. But that's not the way I see it. I believe it springs from the need to take ownership of adult decisions in young urban individuals. And 'love' in association with marriage has always suggested the existence of an element of conscious choice. In love marriages, one can't blame the parents for lack of application of mind; one takes full ownership of one's decision and its attendant consequences. Hence the need for New Indians to distance themselves from the idea of arranged marriages.

However, ownership of even the most traditional arranged marriages also has changed substantially, for such marriages are increasingly powered by matrimonial portals ensuring that those who choose this method play an active role in the screening and shortlisting of potential partners. While the final decision may be left to 'elders', the need to participate in and hence own the process is strongly experienced.

As I see it, there are a few other ways in which the New Indian Marriage differs from the Old Indian Marriage. For instance, a young architect couple recently told me that both of them had, and continue to have, high expectations of each other, even if some of these are irrational. Neither is at all averse to expressing these strongly and demanding that these be responded to by their partner. Also, they are much more emotionally expressive and sexually experimenting than their parents. Although a third of all marriages have always experienced one form or another of infidelity, young couples tend to do so much earlier (sometimes, as in the case of this architect couple, even a year into the marriage). And while their parents were more discreet about their affairs, younger people are generally more brazen, take higher risks and are much more likely to have their affairs discovered by their partners. Friends seem to play as important a role in their lives and marriages as their families do. And, unlike their parents, they are not so recalcitrant about seeking professional help to resolve their differences (frighteningly, their primary source of referral to marriage counsellors is Google). And finally, divorce is no longer a dirty word in their lexicons and minds.

However, when it comes to the way they conduct their marriages, they may not actually be too different from their forebears. A young couple I recently met, married for three and a half years, she a copywriter and he a client service executive in the same advertising agency, was understandably loath to agree with this line of thought. Although they expressed that they don't think of marriage as a sacrament, neither was comfortable when her sister decided to walk out of a highly toxic and violent marriage, for they believed that she should have hung in there for at least a few more years, and been patient with her husband, because in many other ways he was a 'good' guy. Of course they baulked at the thought of marriage being a contract, but both were very wary when it came to financial transparency with each other, for 'this was not what they'd signed up for'. Also, their tendency to 'keep score', of the unfulfilled promises made to each other, seem to indicate otherwise. Although they professed to viewing their marriage as an equal relationship between two people, the power equations in their marriage were quite lopsided and his chauvinism was accepted as a fact of life as was her having to take primary responsibility of managing the home, besides her job. To reiterate, the New Indian Marriage has not quite decided what precisely it should look like. At the moment it seems, to me at least, that the New Indian does want marriage to be different and more exciting, but is not yet ready to define it in more specific terms.

However, I do believe that this redefinition will become clearer over the next couple of decades, if not earlier. Towards achieving this goal, the most significant challenge that the New Indian Marriage is likely to face will be in managing the impact of the family on the marriage. Sadly, in contemporary life, the biggest stress factor on the marriage is the impact of the family. From my experience, I have no doubt that the family's concerns are all genuine and come from a good place. However, in attempting to protect their children from the vagaries of marital dynamics, parents often end up, even if inadvertently, making matters much more difficult to manage, particularly when said children are struggling to create a viable marriage space for themselves, as happened when a mother-in-law recently suggested to her son-in-law that he should use ribbed condoms rather than expecting her daughter to take the contraceptive pill. I'm not suggesting that families should be abandoned by couples. But I do believe that marriage spaces need to be clearly delineated from family spaces, for only then can the integrity of the marriage be maintained. Otherwise it is bound to haplessly remain, as it has for centuries, a subset of the family, an unfortunate scenario as history and experience has taught us.

The other big hurdle that the New Indian Marriage will have to overcome is in creating a reasonably equal balance between partners. While I do believe that no two individuals can be completely equal all the time, the balance cannot afford to perpetually tilt in one direction, more so when the reason for this is attributable to chromosomal factors. The stereotype of the dominant, chauvinistic male has inevitably resulted in the emergence of its bête noir – the stereotype of the Alpha Female. For as long as the alpha position is seen as the coveted one, marriage will be more of a political equation than a nurturing relationship. There is enough evidence to suggest that the desire to find the equitable prototype is keenly experienced and that the quest for this is well under way.

Only time will tell how the New Indian Marriage manages to find a nice bridge between the Old Indian Marriage, which always emphasized that marriage was between two families than two individuals, and the modern egocentric marriage, where the families are actively extruded from the marriage space. I'm confident that it will. I'm also confident that when it does, it's not going to be a pale imitation of the Western marriage or, indeed, any other form of marriage. It's going to be distinct and unique – not quite a sacrament, not really a contract, but more of a conscious relationship between two mindful adults; well delineated, though not alienated, from the family and the social background it's a part of.

About the Contributors

Sharanya Manivannan is the author of the critically acclaimed short-story collection *The High Priestess Never Marries*, which won the 2016 South Asia Laadli Media and Advertising Award for Gender Sensitivity in the category of Best Book (Fiction). She is also the author of two books of poetry, *Witchcraft* and *The Altar of the Only World*, and a children's picture book, *The Ammuchi Puchi*. Her long-running column 'The Venus Flytrap' appears in the *New Indian Express*. Sharanya was specially commissioned to write and perform a poem at the 2015 Commonwealth Day Observance at Westminster Abbey, London. Her poetry, fiction and essays have been widely published internationally. She was born in India in 1985 and grew up in Sri Lanka and Malaysia.

Chitra Viraraghavan was educated in Hyderabad, Kodaikanal, Madras and Boston. She has worked in academic publishing, taught English, and is a book editor, school textbook writer, author of *The Americans: A Novel*, and co-editor of *Madras on My Mind: A City in Stories*. She is working on her second book, a work of historical fiction. *Delhi Thaatha: A Great Grand Story*, a children's book about a philosopher, is forthcoming.

Rita Mukherjee had been weaving stories ever since she could remember. In her youth they got her out of trouble with her teachers and parents. As a senior citizen, terminally ill with lung fibrosis, her stories helped her find solace and keep her sanity intact while pushing her illness back. Her stories have been published on the web, at sulekha.com, sitagita.com, womennova.com, Kala Kahani; in newspapers and magazines; by Children's Book Trust; and in an Indian edition of Chicken Soup for the Soul. Her wit didn't leave her even when she was diagnosed with a life-threatening disease and was given a year. Her husband, Amit, stole another ten from God and medical science. Rita passed away in 2017.

Krishna Shastri Devulapalli is a humour writer, cartoonist, columnist and the quintessential Madras–Chennai novelist. His first novel *Ice Boys in Bell-bottoms* is a chronicle of a 1970s childhood in the city while *Jump Cut* is a serio-comic thriller with the Madras film industry as its backdrop. His comic epistolary play, *Dear Anita*, sends up the Indian publishing industry, as does a work of non-fiction, *How to be a Literary Sensation*. His most recent novel is *The Sentimental Spy: The Family Bond*. He is the co-editor of the anthology *Madras on My Mind: A City in Stories*.

Prasoon Joshi is an Indian lyricist, screenwriter, poet and marketer. He is the CEO of McCann World group India, a subsidiary of global marketing firm McCann Erickson. On 11 August 2017, he was appointed the chairperson of the Central Board of Film Certification. He has received the Filmfare Best

Lyricist Award three times, in 2007 and 2008 and most recently in 2014 for the Hindi movie *Bhaag Milkha Bhaag*. He also received the National Film Award for Best Lyrics twice, for his work in *Taare Zameen Par* (2007), and *Chittagong* (2013). He was awarded Padma Shri by the Government of India in 2015, for his contributions towards the field of arts, literature and advertising.

Noor Zaheer is a writer and researcher, writing in English, Hindi and Urdu. Important published works include *My God Is a Woman*, which won the Foundation of SAARC Writers Literary Award; *Silent Dunes*; *Raging Forests* (short-story collection); *Mere Hisse ki Roshnai*, which won the Delhi Hindi Academy Award; *Surkh Karavan ke Hamsafar* in Hindi [travelogue]; *Ret Par Khoon*, a short-story collection in Urdu; *Patthar ke Sainik* (a drama); *Aaj ke Naam*, a biography of Faiz Ahmed Faiz; and *The Dancing Lama*.

Her latest book, *Denied by Allah!*, discusses the medieval laws, sexist bias and maintenance of tradition and conventions in the name of Islam, and questions the archaic laws and patriarchy in a democratic set-up.

Kalyan Ray's family was uprooted from the Ganges Delta (now Bangladesh) through a combination of political upheavals and natural disasters. He was born and grew up in Calcutta. Educated in India and the US, he has taught on three continents, in Ecuador, Jamaica and the Philippines where he was a visiting professor of comparative theology. He has long been associated with Indian social service organizations, and collaborated with Mother Teresa, translating and voice-acting for the first documentary on her. He is the author of the novels *Eastwords* and *No Country*, and is currently completing his third novel, *Heaven and Earth*. He is married to film-maker and actor Aparna Sen, and lives now in India.

Harimohan Paruvu played first-class cricket for Hyderabad and was a banker before he turned into a columnist, blogger, executive coach, teacher and writer. He has authored four books and has contributed to a sports anthology *Let's Play*. His first novel *The Men Within – A Cricketing Tale* was made into a Telugu movie *Golconda High School*. His second book was a novel *If You Love Someone...* which was followed by *50 Not Out – 50 Lessons from Cricket* and *This Way Is Easier Dad – How My Daughter Saved Me from Growing Up*. He lives in Hyderabad with his wife, Shobha, and daughter, Anjali.

He has long been associated with Indian social service organizations, and collaborated with Mother Teresa, translating and voice-acting for the first documentary on her. He is married to film-maker and actress, Aparna Sen.

Deeksha Nagar is an ethnographer and a folklorist with extensive experience in the field of community education and multiculturalism. In early 1990s, Deeksha began working in creative education in India, co-authoring teaching and learning materials with the help of community members who had been deprived of formal literacy. Since earning her PhD in folklore from Indiana University, Deeksha has served as the curator of Education at the Mathers Museum of World Cultures at Indiana University and taught anthropology at University of Northern Colorado. Currently Deeksha is engaged in literary and cultural projects rooted in collaborative models of research and activism that address issues of education, immigration, cultural preservation. As a passionate and uniquely skilled writer in Hindi and English, she has published articles, book chapters and curated exhibits on folklore, foodlore and American life.

Neha Dixit is an independent journalist based in New Delhi, India. She covers politics, gender and social justice in South

Asia. She has reported for Al Jazeera, Smithsonian, the *Caravan*, the *New York Times*, *Outlook* and several other media and publications. She has contributed to the UNESCO Global Casebook of Investigative Journalism 2011, Zubaan Anthology on Sexual Violence in South Asia and *First Hand: Graphic Non-Fiction in India*. She has won multiple awards, including Kurt Schork Award in International Journalism, 2014; Lorenzo Natali Prize for Journalism from the European Commission, 2011; and Chameli Devi Jain Award for Outstanding Woman Journalist in India, 2017; among others.

Bulbul Sharma is a painter and writer whose works are in the collection of the National Gallery of Modern Art, Lalit Kala Akademi and Chandigarh Museum, as well as in private collections in India, UK, US, Japan, Canada and France. Her books include *My Sainted Aunts*, *Anger of Aubergines*, *Banana Flower Dreams*, *Eating* Women, *Telling Tales Now that I am Fifty*, *Tailor of Giripul* and *Grey Hornbills at Dusk*, besides children's books. Her books have been translated into Italian, French, German, Chinese, Spanish and Finnish. Bulbul conducts 'storypainting' workshops for special needs children and is a founder and member of Sannidhi, an NGO that works in village schools in the Himachal mountains.

Modhurima Sinha – journalist, photographer, author – has written on films and photography for many years (*Femina*, *Telegraph* and *Asian Photography*) and has assisted noted Indian film-maker Aparna Sen on several of her films and renowned American photographer Laura McPhee. Modhurima has directed one short film – *The Third Eye* – which has travelled across the world to Athens, Cypress, Stockholm, Dhaka, Los Angeles, Toronto, Houston, Bhutan, to name a few. Her first feature film, *Talking of Michelangelo*, recently premiered at The Kolkata International Film Festival. Her day job as the director of public relations at the Taj Bengal keeps her occupied, but she still manages to write whenever she gets time. *Call of the Real*, her book on eleven master painters of Bengal, was published by Mapin in 2003. She lives in Kolkata with her husband and son.

Abha Iyengar is an award-winning, internationally published poet, author, editor and translator. She is a British Council–certified creative writing mentor. Her story 'The High Stool' was nominated for the *storySouth* Million Writers Award. She received the Lavanya Sankaran Writing Fellowship for 2009–2010. Her stories were shortlisted in the DNA Out of Print Contest (2015) and The Strands International Short Story Competition (2017). Her poem-film *Parwaaz* won a Special Jury Prize in Patras, Greece. Her published works include *Yearnings*, *Flash Bites*, *Shrayan*, *Many Fish to Fry* and *The Gourd Seller and Other Stories*. She has co-edited an anthology, *The Other*.

Mumbai-born **Wendell Rodricks** studied fashion designing in the US and France, from 1986 to 1988. Wendell's first collection from Goa earned him the title 'Guru of Minimalism', and his next collection in 1995 pioneered the concept of 'resort wear' and 'eco-friendly' garments, at a time when the words were not yet known in India.

In 2010 Wendell revived the weaving of the traditional Goan Kunbi sari, a two-year project involving identifying and training weavers in the use of sari looms. His book *Moda Goa – History and Style*, published by HarperCollins, got rave reviews for its portrayal of long-forgotten aspects of Goa's cultural and sartorial history. He has authored two other books, *The Green Room* and *Poksem*.

In 2014, the designer was awarded India's fourth highest civilian honour, the Padma Shri, and he has won other awards including Knight in the Order of Arts and Letters (Chevalier de l'Ordre National des Arts et Lettres) by The Ministry of Culture and Communication of France.

Milan Vohra is a juggler. She juggles writing fiction and ad campaigns. She juggles writing novels and short stories. She juggles writing romances that involve tall, dark broody men (in her first book, the first Indian Mills & Boon, *The Love Asana*), mixed-up millennials with multiple piercings and as many relationship issues (in her latest novel *Tick Tock We're 30*), and pious Indian people who have relationships with their agarbattis (in ad land). She juggles living between Delhi and Bengaluru, with pit stops in Mumbai.

Vijay Nagaswami is a Chennai-based psychiatrist and has worked closely with relationships for over three and a half decades. Innumerable couples from all over the country have benefitted from his marital interventions and his writings. He has written six books, including the bestselling New Indian Marriage series published by Westland Books. He also wrote a column for the *Hindu* called 'The Shrinking Universe', and his writings have featured in other national and regional publications as well. He can be contacted at vijay.nagaswami@gmail.com

Acknowledgements

To start, I must acknowledge the patience of all contributors to this anthology, which has indeed taken a long time to find its way into print. Thank you, each and every one of you, for not asking 'Are we there yet?'

Only one regret. My friend, whom I met as a student at my writing course, and later befriended, is not with us to read her name and writing in this anthology. Her essay, 'A Life Sentence', talks about her irrevocable health condition. Despite all the care lavished on her by her husband and family, it got the better of her. To Rita Mukherjee, I owe an apology.

I am happy that Karthika V.K. entrusted me with putting together an anthology on marriage.

Thanks too to Shantanu Ray Chaudhuri and Shreya Punj for taking the publication of the book in hand and getting it moving, and to Joseph Antony for his painstaking and meticulous editing, even right through the Christmas holidays.

My thanks also to Ashutosh Jha for his wonderful help styling the book.

And finally, thank you HarperCollins India for this opportunity. It is the first exercise of this kind for me, and has been a learning experience. And that, as we all know, is something to treasure.